The Condition of
the Witness

Jean-Pierre Jossua

SCM PRESS LTD

Translated by John Bowden from the French
La condition du témoin,
published by Les Éditions du Cerf, Paris 1984.

© Les Éditions du Cerf 1984

Translation © John Bowden 1985

Jossua, Jean-Pierre
  The condition of the witness.
  1. Witness bearing (Christianity)
  I. Title   II. La condition du témoin. *English*
  248'.5   BV4520

  ISBN 0-334-01960-5

                    334 01960 5

            First published in English 1985
                  by SCM Press Ltd
            26-30 Tottenham Road, London N1

        Phototypeset by Input Typesetting Ltd
            and printed in Great Britain by
         Richard Clay (The Chaucer Press) Ltd
                  Bungay, Suffolk

Contents

Preface *by Nicholas Lash, Norris-Hulse Professor of Divinity
in the University of Cambridge*   v

1 What do we mean by witnessing? A new approach
   to an old question   1

   Witness and witnessing   1
   The Time of Patience and its consequences   3
   Taking up the questioning again   7

2 If we have to talk of God   12

   Summoning witnesses   12
   Producing a resonance   15
   Orientation for a quest   20
   Choosing a language   24

3 The basic interpretation of Christian witness   29

   Flight from the world   29
   The incarnation   32
   An integrally human Christianity   35
   Questions of vocabulary   40
   Witnessing and the church   43

4 The experience of the witness   48

   Themes of witness   48
   His assurance   50
   His particularity   51
   The witnessing community   53
   Solitude and failure   55
   The witness, condition for God   58
   The presence of the witness   60
   The genesis of faith in witnessing   63

5 Relations between believers and non-Christians   65

   Believers: removing some misunderstandings   65
   Believers: some conditions for another approach   70
   Non-believers: some attitudes to faith or to Christians   74

6 Witness and witnessing in the church   81
   Who is a witness for his companions on the way?   81
   Building one another up within the community   85
   The goal of witnessing   87

Preface

The English Channel is a great deal wider than the North Sea, at least where theological communication is concerned. Most British readers of theology could run off a long list of theologians working in Germany, a list which might include such names as Moltmann and Küng, Pannenberg and Metz, Hengel and Jüngel. And although we cannot pronounce Schillebeeckx's name, we have heard of it. But the French? They are far further off. Therefore although, as Gifford Lecturer in Edinburgh in 1977, Père Jossua is not quite a stranger to these islands, he needs a word of introduction.

Jean-Pierre Jossua, the child of an agnostic Jewish family, studied medicine in Paris, where he was born in 1930. In 1952 he was converted to Christianity, joining the Dominican order in 1953. Pursuing theological studies in Paris and Strasbourg, he was fortunate enough to count amongst his friends and teachers two outstanding colleagues: Marie-Dominique Chenu and Yves Congar (of whom he published a brief intellectual biography in 1965). For nearly ten years he was Professor of Dogmatic Theology and Rector of the house of studies in Paris (a hundred yards from where another Dominican, Thomas Aquinas, had taught some time before). Since 1970 he has been co-director of the Fundamental Theology section of the journal *Concilium*, and has recently taken on responsibility for editing the review *Etudes Freudiennes*.

In the early 1970s, becoming disillusioned with purely 'academic' theology, Père Jossua began to explore ways in which a more direct account could be given of Christian experience: a project which entailed the labour of seeking to renew and purify our religious language. This project bore fruit in a series of studies of which *The Condition of the Witness* is the most recent.

French Dominican theology in the twentieth century has never been confined to an 'ivory tower'. The order was expelled from France in 1905 and, not long after its return, thirty years later, found itself under pressure now not from political but ecclesiastical authorities. Chenu, who had sent students to work down the mines, and had drawn up a programme of study which indicated clearly the connections between living theology and social change, was removed from office as rector of the house of studies, while Congar, who had spent part of the war in Colditz, was forbidden to teach and spent an enforced sabbatical year in Cambridge. In quest of the unity of experience and reflection, 'praxis' and understanding, 'engagement' has long been a watchword for French Dominican theology.

An earlier study by Jossua and two of his colleagues, *Une Foi Exposée* (1972), contained an appendix on the notion of 'experience'. In this country, 'religious experience' is often understood in terms of subjective, inner states of feeling, fostering the illusion that we can, as individuals, be 'transparent' to ourselves. This is not an illusion to which someone as steeped as Jossua is in the thought of Hegel, Kierkegaard and Freud, would be likely to fall victim. For him, the attempt to render an account of our Christian experience – as people with particular patterns of culture, politics, memory, friendship and suffering – is itself a constitutive aspect of the living reality which it seeks to 'refract', interpret, render articulate in conversation.

The redirection of Père Jossua's work, away from the language of the textbooks and the learned journals, would be misunderstood if it were taken to be a shift from the rigorous to the relaxed, from the technical to the popular. As I understand what he is trying to do, it is a matter not so much of popularization as of *distillation*. There is a density in this book, demanding patience, effort and reflection from the reader. But it is the density of the poetic, of a simplicity which renders richness accessible.

There are several references in this book to an earlier study, *Le Temps de la Patience* (1976), which treated of similar themes, covered much of the same ground, but did so more schematically, more abstractly. That book was written in collaboration; this one is more personal, more autobiographical, and hence more concrete.

One of the striking things about this book is the unification it achieves between theology and spirituality, enquiry and contemplation. Hence the stillness, the tranquillity, the *courtesy* of the prose. Christian witness is so often noisy and aggressive: 'The professional witness is a public and private menace'. In this book, nobody is hectored or browbeaten. Jossua suggests that the starting-point of dialogue with those for whom the negative description 'non-believer' merely serves to absolve us from the need seriously to attend to their convictions may often be 'an honest probing of disillusionment', of shared unease, in the pain and confusion of our culture. We are constrained to bear witness; we have no alternative but to seek to give an account of the hope that is in us. And we find it impossible to do so. We have no language that is not 'heard' (by others, and perhaps often by ourselves) to say almost the *opposite* of what we *want* to say. Perhaps we try too hard, talk too much, and live too little. We might try attentiveness and stillness; filled silence, in which the other person (whom we thought it our duty to address) may enable us to bring that hope to speech. The initiative is not with us, though we bear responsibility for the task of witnessing, but with the other – and with God: 'A blank space in the text, a patch of silence, a sudden pause while talking ought to be the first introduction of God into speech or writing.' That, perhaps, is how the eloquent silence of God takes flesh, finds form, in what we took to be our emptiness.

Nicholas Lash

1

What do we mean by witnessing?
A new approach to an old question

Witness and witnessing

I am one of those believers whose delight in the faith inevitably makes me want to communicate it. So I find it particularly necessary to reflect on the condition of the witness. That is something I can only do in the way which has become second nature to me, describing experience and looking at it critically, without claiming that this approach brings out all aspects of the problem.

The word 'condition' has a wealth of different connotations. It evokes a complex of specific characteristics: we talk about the 'human condition', but also about our present condition, as opposed to the past. The term also prompts a number of basic questions. What are the conditions for witnessing? Is the presence of witnesses truly a condition for the manifestation of God?

I do not see the witness as someone who takes the initiative in speaking to others. I see the witness, rather, as a man or woman living in such a way – and looking at the world and everything in it in such a way – as to make other people ask themselves, and ask those who are witnesses, what gives them their unique character. In using the word 'unique', I do not mean to suggest that witnessing calls for actions or thoughts of absolute originality which can be recognized as such by friends. It is enough for witnesses to display certain unexpected resources by which they can live, or help others in coping with their lives; indeed, witnesses may simply combine in their persons a significant set of characteristics, none of which is in itself specifically new. Such character-istics might include goodness, joy in prayer, continuing hope in humanity, along with full awareness of all the reasons for despair.

I do not attach any importance to an 'efficient' kind of witnessing which affirms itself at the expense of its authenticity. In my view – and I shall return to this point more than once – authenticity can only be achieved if what is supremely at stake in faith is approached through the complexities of real human existence, with its demands, its opportunities and its trials. That is where faith is to be sought; not in exceptional conditions which allow people to by-pass whole areas of life, allegedly in order to draw nearer to the 'divine', either through detachment or through sacrifice. For in fact the 'divine' is manifested only through incarnation and love which involves itself in our condition.

Believers and unbelievers alike have been constantly fascinated by this dream of a kind of immediate presence of the Absolute which makes its mark on human beings who have been scrubbed clean of their human characteristics. However, it not only tends to produce false witnessing through its orientation on a perverse image of God, but also proves to be a delusion. This can easily be seen by looking at the sort of lives which people have thought they could make for themselves in this way: the realities they thought they had escaped have nevertheless continued to shape them. The only exceptions are some sublime short-cuts over which I would not presume to set myself up in judgment. Because witnessing is a communal condition, the witness is to some degree anonymous; nevertheless, even though individuals may be swal-lowed up in the crowd, if they respond, bit by bit, to what is offered, it is as individuals that they will be surrounded by the radiance marking the passing of 'God', almost imperceptible yet supremely glorious.

Some Christians have had to navigate too many obstacles to show clear signs of the victory of a humane faith, even when they have in fact achieved it. To this degree the integrity of their witness – in the sense indicated above – remains fragile. Perhaps they might be compared with others who, conversely, have been wounded by not having overcome quickly enough the slowness and uncertainty in their discovery of God. I would like to think that paying such a price or experiencing such difficulties simply makes the end-result all the more significant. However, that is not how the world sees it; once again, for the world the miracle is the important thing, even if it is a pseudo-miracle or, more precisely, an empty one.

To speak only of the former group, in which I would include myself: given the chance, the disquiet involved in meeting the intrinsic demands of witnessing can lead a person to devote his or her energies to the effort of thinking and writing. Now of course in one way, a book proves nothing. If the author has no talent, it gets nowhere; if he or she has only a little, things are worse, because it is never possible to get away completely from the delusion of magnifying something which barely exists by the magic of words. Even those who claim to be no more than 'poets of the religious', celebrating the possible beauty of something in which they do not really dare to claim a share, can be denounced as a peddling illusions. In short, only the trace of a Presence, sensed in the reality of existence, can prompt questions.

But that is not the whole story. Those who have both a certain gift and an authentic experience may find that living out their faith in everyday life, which is a necessary condition of witness, goes along with a gift for writing, producing a combination of integrity and power of conviction.

The Time of Patience and its consequences

In *The Time of Patience*, which I and some colleagues wrote in 1976, we stressed the incomprehensible, scandalous distance between the meaning and value of faith, what those who have experience recognize as its contribution to human life, and the way in which such people find it almost completely impossible to communicate that faith. This is a dilemma which people may find themselves in when the illusions and 'missionary' phraseology on which they have been fed for thirty years eventually become void of content.

Our book described how witnessing has to take a very long way round when it is understood as sharing an existence in the course of which (one hopes) the vitality of the good news of Jesus could again become evident, in a world which, though not

3

evangelized, is a post-Christian world. It takes this course, whether in order to help in coping with problems common to all human beings or in order to raise questions which have been forgotten. We also showed there that our responsibility as witnesses only goes as far as offering our experience in a way which respects human freedom and the ways of God, without ulterior motives, and without even a thought of 'conversion'.

We mentioned two ways of reducing a profound unease – a bad conscience, even a crisis of identity – brought on among Christians once they had been rudely awakened to the failure of their missionary verve. In our view, now is the time when discretion, silence, a tentative quest for a life-style and way of thought in keeping with the enormity of the difference between our day and the Christian past, hold out more promise for the future than spectacular demonstrations, public declarations, and the claim always to have known everything. But in that case how do we escape a feeling of dumbness and anonymity which, if not permanent, are at least extremely persistent?

We felt that we should safeguard the possibility of describing our experience at the very point where it continued to be impossible for us to formulate what we believed, either because the questions addressed to us were not mature enough or because the language in which we restated the confession of faith was too advanced. It is important to talk about the many facets of Christian experience of which we have a reflective and critical awareness, for this is an experience which can be discussed and to some degree verified. The distance between this faith lived out in experience and the symbols of faith (in both senses of the word) is not unbridgable, not least because the experiences are the active interpretation of the symbols and the symbols are at best themselves simply the inspired expression of fundamental experiences.

We also suggested that whereas the isolated witness runs the risk of seeing his or her most significant actions or judgments ultimately in terms of his or her personal 'truth', witnessing by Christian communities – supposedly brought into being by faith and in need of faith to expand – should have a clearer direction. That is, provided that there are communities capable of this, and

4

that their social conditioning is not even more ambiguous than the psychologies of individuals; provided that such communities are not so self-contradictory that they cancel one another out. There are so many 'ifs' – but I do know some fine examples.

Another set of reflections can also alter the suffering and the scandal arising from the impossibility of communicating faith, from the rapid diminution of the churches by reason of the gulf which divides the generations, and more generally from the very small number of Christians in comparison to the extent of humanity in space and time. In the end, it is a matter of accepting Christianity as a particular historical current, one which will remain precisely that, even if we take into account the authenticity of its gospel and do not see it simply as a religious ideology of the West.

So I would understand Christianity as a faith which, by proclaiming the gospel and the power of the resurrection, reveals and gives new force to the meaning of the 'creation' and 'salvation' of the world (though if we understand these properly, they are one and the same thing, the second word denoting a new creation for us). Because these things come from God, they open up unlimited hope. However, even so Christianity would only be the visible crest of an enormous ground-swell through which God constantly stirs up our human waves.

Thus the 'new people of God', of whom the Bible speaks and who becomes the subject of the universal and definitive 'new covenant', is not the totality of Christians, far less the church, but humanity as a whole. They are those to whom 'the kingdom of God' is promised and for whom it does not cease to come, if it is welcomed, infiltrating them and eventually bowling them over. While it may be true that Jesus preached only to Jews, the universality of his message is bound up with the profound humanity of the relationship which he inaugurates: he challenges the temple, makes the law relative. offers unconditional pardon and restoration, and shows us that everyone is our neighbour. On this point the disciples understood him well.

So there is only one sense in which Christianity can be absolute, and of universal appeal: what appears with it is everyone's concern. It must bear witness in humility to what its outward insignificance makes paradoxical and almost unbelievable: God has revealed his secret in Jesus Christ in a way which cannot be surpassed.

I have not taken over anything or anyone: historical events and human beings are what they are, what they seek to be and claim to be; I do not make them either seek God or find God against their will. To put what I believe quite simply: my God himself seeks them, and doubtless finds them, by ways of which I have no knowledge. At most, hearing the gospel and observing life sometimes allow me to sense some points of convergence.

Similarly, my views are quite free of any trace of a theology of history: I have spoken of 'meaning' in terms of significance, not of direction. Creation, gospel, resurrection, kingdom come about anywhere, at any time. I have nothing against evolution running its course, inexorable progress, the great drifts of history, the signs of the times – however, there are no longer many arguments in their favour; so I have chosen the punctiliar one.

Some of the preceding reflections tend to play down the originality of Christian behaviour, while others convey a hope that the act of bearing witness might find a foundation in the questioning that they evoke. And if we simply consider the ethical sphere, where the problem is most acute, is there really a contradiction here?

Suppose we accept that there is nothing absolutely distinctive in the behaviour I have just mentioned – was what formerly seemed to be distinctive Christian behaviour really so original? Did it derive from revelation or from the social environment of Christians? Did it not vary considerably? Had it not been incorporated in our cultural heritage for a very long time? And in any case, is that not what we might expect if we allow that God the saviour is also the creator, and if we reject the semi-Manichaean fantasy of a humanity steeped in evil?

However, the morality of the best human beings and that of the world as it is are two very different things: institutions and law may make progress, but new social perversions appear. A society may become more refined in its sensibilities and yet in other respects produce the fruits of injustice and murder. That is why if Christians live out the demands which the message of the

Bible makes on them in relationships and social responsibilities – without passing too rapidly over the psychological or economic components of these demands or failing to recognize the difficulties of historical situations – their actions will not go unheeded; what becomes familiar through constant repetition sometimes remains new and surprising when it is actually put into practice.

Taking up the questioning again

I have been reflecting for twelve years on the gap there is between the strength and the joy of the faith within me, within us, and the brick wall which Christian witnessing comes up against. Over that time, the perspectives which I have outlined should have mitigated my sense of disquiet, the impression of meaningless-ness that I had felt. However, I have to confess that nothing of the sort has happened. In a sense, I am still at the same point.

The fact is that my most basic motive for witnessing did not stem from a compulsion to 'save' others, from the hope of swelling the ranks of the church, from the illusion that it is enough to speak well, from the vanity of believing that success could depend on us, or even from the anxiety which is soothed by unanimity, the blame which guiltily attributes failure to a lack of holiness. It arose out of the very experience of faith, the very idea of God which had made its mark on me.

It is the quality, the intensity, the duration of the good things that I have received from the gospel which make me want to show them to others and which torment me by their apparent insignificance, by the increasing indifference which I encounter when I try to convey them. I do not understand what happens. Moreover, because I am increasingly convinced of the greatness of God and therefore that anyone can go to him without being demeaned, I find aberrant the either-or which dominates our culture: you have to opt for either the dignity and happiness of man or the knowledge of God. I agonize for God and for those people who believe this to be the case.

If you are ready to drink the cup of bitterness in a situation to

7

the end, you may find mixed in with it a touch of gentleness and clarity.

Anyone who reflects on witnessing will come up against a number of different elements. There will be the basic, lasting characteristics which every Christian witness must have experienced since the beginnings of our faith, and others connected with our specific situation in the 'developed' West. Now this situation does not seem to me to be utterly new: what is original about it could well be that that we are faced with the purest and most disturbing conditions for bearing witness that followers of Jesus have ever encountered. I am well aware that in every age Christians have had a tendency to think that theirs was the most significant situation. But the difficulty that we feel is perhaps an indication of an exceptional kind of integrity that is required of us. And at the same time it raises a formidable question. Do not its ambiguities bring the possibility of witnessing to an end?

From the fourth to the eighteenth century, Christianity was handed down from one generation to another in an almost infallible way through education in the family, the parish or the school, and this ensured the persistence of a religion which had many social functions (just how important they were can be seen from the pressure which society exerted in the other direction). This made it possible for conversions to the gospel to happen time and again – far too often to calculate. Since at that time the world was nominally Christian, witnessing was a call to become an effective Christian; relations with the 'others', within Christianity or outside it, were almost always characterized by the exercising of temporal power, not to say violence.

Since the eighteenth century, this complex has fallen apart. The classical functions of Christianity disappeared, leaving aside spectacular local revivals like those in middle-class France in the second half of the nineteenth century or in Poland in the twentieth. This same development also meant that the pressure to conform was so reduced that whether or not Christian parents had Christian children was purely a matter of chance. Everything depended on the psychological make-up of individuals and whether or not the generation gap was overcome. Of course 'missions' played their part with varying degrees of success; however, no matter what, they experienced the recoil from an earlier exercise of power by Christianity.

In some cases Christianity rediscovered a different kind of social relevance: it was the inspiration behind development, a challenge to unjust political and economic structures. There is no doubt that this is more in keeping with its original, authentic character. However, such a development did not remove the doubts which afflicted it and which quickly rebounded against Christian belief: a failure to recognize the radical difference between contemporary culture and biblical times, or the tendency to by-pass the many intermediary disciplines needed to form a bridge between past and present.

In our Western context, it might be argued that from about 1730 Christians and non-Christians were opposed in a way which had a parallel only in the days before the elimination of ancient paganism. They came up against each other relatively freely. However, modern conditions are very different from those of antiquity.

For a long time, given the weight of the past, not to mention the persistence of an authoritarian control of the church in its cultural environment, those who were not Christians were also anti-Christians or at least the leading figures in an anti-clerical struggle which, for all the more positive virtues that we can see today, nevertheless muddied the waters when it came to witnessing. This is a factor whose days are numbered, but our contemporaries remain post-Christians – a fact which cannot be stressed enough. They already 'know'; they are convinced that they have all the answers.

Even supposing that the memory of Christendom faded and a new perspective on the church became possible, there would be another way in which our situation is quite new. From the first to the fourth centuries, the Christian faith was proclaimed in a religious world: it showed how different it was – very clearly, to begin with, then less so as it was affected by the interplay of reciprocal influences and the pressures of a common situation. However, no one challenged its importance. Today, however, it has to exist and proclaim the whole of its experience and its message without support from our culture: it can presuppose nothing, and indeed more often than not has itself to raise the questions to which it hopes to give an answer.

Nor is that the whole story. The established presence of the other great religions does not help; indeed, it distracts attention and is an inducement to relativism, perhaps even a global challenge. So it is easy to see how perhaps for the first time in history the Christian is absolutely naked, with no support from society, with no possibility of appealing to a religious sense, reduced to carrying his own baggage – if that is the right word for this strange wealth which could also be called poverty. Yes, for the very first time the Christian bears unambiguous witness to his or her God.

The reason why I have raised the question of witnessing once again stems from my concern to explore more fully the utter lack of resources available to the witness. What does it mean today, in my relations with my unbelieving friends, to be a witness of the constant proximity of 'God', of whose very existence they are unaware, which they even deny?

The complexity of the question arises from the fact that more is at stake than presenting a spiritual itinerary. Witnessing is related to the discovery of God as the happiness and ultimate truth of human beings brought about through Jesus Christ – without denying anything of the possibility and the authenticity of a human life without God. This involves the hypothesis of an allegiance to Christianity. Yet Christianity is so varied and so contrasting. What position do I take? How do I present it to others? How do I commit myself to an idealistic venture which will never be realized? How do I go back on what for me has always been, and is, a privileged approach?

Reflecting on faith from the perspective of witnessing, I do not find myself arriving at a kind of last chapter which discusses how much there is to communicate. This again is something that I am trying to discover, to understand, to live out, at the very moment when I am asking myself how to communicate it. For me all these questions are one and the same thing – and indeed they are probably also intrinsically one and the same. What do I know of the word understood as the response which arises within myself apart from what has appeared on my lips, in my actions or in my books?

10

What I want to do is to spend some time going over a number of the intrinsic difficulties in this question, well aware that they cannot be clarified or even expressed by means of a simple reflective approach. The topics we consider might well include the language in which one tries to 'say' God, Christianity as a specific choice, the intrinsic structure of the act of witnessing, the contemporary relationship between believers and non-Christians, and perhaps also that of the role of witnessing in the reciprocal development of faith between believers. Other issues are bound to arise as I write, even if so far they have not yet come to mind.

2

If we have to talk of God

One afternoon, 'God' imprinted himself on my mind as an infinite personal presence with whom I could converse. My life has been changed several times since, but He has not shifted.

At that time I was living in an existential wilderness: nothing made sense. It was also a time of psychological crisis: without knowing it, I was looking for a way out.

I picked up a book which spoke to God as though he were an intimate friend with utter, burning conviction, and in an elevated literary style which was intended to move me. This approach produced such an upheaval within me that I found myself caught up in the prayer that I was reading.

What I felt, my 'experience' in the strict sense, was important – but it was also ambiguous; it would be unwise to attach supreme importance to something extremely fragile. In the light of what followed, the essential thing seems to me to be that here faith aroused faith: I had been enabled to believe, and I had wanted to believe, longed to believe.

I think that I could argue that the great image of fatherhood which arose from this experience, soon to be combined with my choice of the 'religious life', allowed me to negotiate smoothly the obstacles which had made this moment in my life so critical. Certainly, however, neither the image nor the choice could have alleviated my problems without making me their prisoner, had not a different approach later led me to find a happy outcome.

Things then seemed to me to make abundant sense; but today I find it difficult to say what that sense was. Since I feel that it is only after the last few years that I have arrived at an understanding of Christianity, to which I am still committed, and since I am aware that others have understood it and still understand it in a different way, I can only conclude that Christianity continues to be fertile, but is capable of a variety of interpretations.

There is one fixed point in these changes: God. I believe that despite efforts to make me see him as a great Being of whom, or in the name of whom, one speaks, I have not completely forgotten that if I did not always speak *to* him, at least implicitly, I would lose him.

I now tend to persuade myself also that what I say and write with my attention focussed on him cannot fail in some way also to be expressed *by* him. Precisely how can we attribute such varied ways of speaking to him, and what are they about? Indeed, to put it slightly differently, is the 'Word of God' ever more than utterances of human beings prompted by him, in which others discover him? Could anyone invoke him, interpret the old words in a new way, bear witness to his nearness, without his being involved? But what are we to make of the countless follies that have been uttered about him?

I can only express the surprise that I feel every day: on the one hand I have come to believe in and understand God by tradition, reflection, experience, numerous authentic facts; on the other I still seem to be confronted with nothing but the unknown and watch all assertions or images disappearing when I try to comprehend what they actually mean. Subtraction never produces anything but this: 'You are, my God'. Apart from that, I know nothing of him.

There are phrases about God in which I put my trust. Here are some of them. He is infinite and personal existence. He abides in his joy and has need of humanity. He has created the world, in the mystery of being. He counters the non-sense of evil with boundless justice. He raises up life beyond death. He makes himself present in human destiny. He lives in our depths through his spirit. But what do they mean? It is sheer illusion to suppose that we can grasp and articulate concepts: and do not symbols or stories in the long run leave thought equally impoverished, if they are directly focussed on the heart of the believer?

Is this not the clearest indication one could ask for that this 'knowing' is not knowledge of anything real? But in that case, to what do we owe the origin and all the consequences of giving one's life for justice, of the endless passion aroused by science, the love of a man and a woman, Cézanne's beloved *Sainte-Victoire*, the posthumous sonatas of Schubert, the *Duino Elegies*? Does the world of the senses reveal all its secrets? Is clarity, thought, the ultimate? Is unconscious desire the only hidden thing?

So the right question to ask might be this. Why, having attained maturity, should one madly commit oneself to detachment, freedom from anything to do with the senses, and reify (by giving it a name, God) the absolute which is never more than intimated, sensed? Such a question is intolerable to anyone who wants to discover, create or quite simply to live by puerility – or, to give it another name, security – and so it gets suppressed. But does not that constrict our very development?

I can only speak for myself: I owe this leap of faith, this vertigo to Him. Either way is difficult, each in its own fashion: but if I allowed this tension to slacken, I think that I would be betraying the light: 'He was amazed when he understood that a God had passed.' So here I am, coming to terms with this word – meditating, writing or going through the daily maze of words and actions – and I cannot, and will not, lay down my arms.

From where has this term God come to me? From Christians. I am convinced that whatever their convictions or claims, all the philosophers who accord God any role other than that of pure hypothesis are theologians, and that they can only sustain their position because of a religion, even though they may have gone beyond it or reinterpreted it. Be this as it may, for my part I know that for me the only effective starting point, indeed the on!y possible one, is the witness of the Hebrew prophets, of Jesus, and of those who have followed in their wake. If I could not put myself in this line, I would find agnosticism inevitable – because I would not have the impudence to claim to be an atheist.

So there is a line of people who claim to be, if not religious geniuses, at least believers. It is a line based on the original experience attested by a revelation or manifestation which still has the power to evoke faith and a kind of derived experience in others. The important thing is that the discovery has always been understood to be something new, a break with our basic knowledge of the world, not something which is part of our real selves and which we have forgotten. In short, it is given and does not arise out of our hearts.

Producing a resonance

However, those who have had this experience have also described it in terms of rediscovering something that they already knew. Would it make sense to us if we did not expect it in some way, or at least if the possibility of its happening were not already there for us in advance? It is not a matter of our searching for it because we are not yet aware that we have in fact found it; nor is it that human life would be nothing without this necessary salvation. In one sense it is optional, addressed to human beings who can stand upright without it; on reflection, it proves to be indispensable for those who have experienced it and recognized all that they could be as a result of it – a paradoxical lack which most often only shows itself in the full flush of success, showing up a great many errors and just as many good attempts.

So are we perhaps talking about a *lack*? Are we talking about the only true rest of the restless heart created for this ecstasy, freedom or action which are hopelessly inadequate without it? Would not the paradox be illuminated if we could describe in terms of an extra gift the experiences stamped on us which allow such an offer to make sense, or subsequently to seem so precious that we never want to let it go? The call of the infinite is understood in a variety of different ways; it is an occasion for human beings to stand upright and continue to create in a finite world, limited though they are. Could this call not also prepare them to listen to the voice which would speak to them as the living Absolute?

No one who has come to know and wonder at the last quartets of Beethoven could say that to be ignorant of them could be a lack or that to discover them would be the fulfilment of a secret expectation. However, the extra dimension that they reveal in

15

their capacity for creating beauty and entering into it with pure emotion is of such a kind that once having discovered them one could never imagine being without them from then on. One would not want to do without them at any price, and cannot but welcome their testimony to the powers that are latent in human beings.

As I meditate in this way on *lack*, I realize again that it is impossible to reflect on faith without asking what there is in us that makes it possible. This is an existential question (how could 'salvation' concern us? – even if the word and the reality have a more positive dimension than the response to a situation of distress). It is also an intellectual question (how can the very idea of God make sense? – and that is rather different from a philosophical approach to the divine). The latter entails a well known difficulty: does it make sense to claim that God has shown himself in history? This is a blow to our reason and our autonomy, or even to our naivety, if one reflects on the constitutive character of our knowledge.

When we ask about the significance of the event on which our faith is based, the place where we must certainly look for the answer is in the quality of our actual experience. It is here that we find the answer to the suspicion that our experience is no more than a fantasy or a social product with many functions: faith in its entirety is the evidence of its own reality and its possibilities. Again, there must be evidence that faith is not suicidal for the most modest and most confident of intellectual ventures and that its significance is not radically different from that of other factors on which our humanity and our cultural heritage are based.

There are deists who have tried to argue that both the Absolute and reason are so exalted that historical evidence, with its frailty and specific character, cannot form the basis of a convincing intellectual approach to them; only reason, which is intrinsically universal and atemporal, has such a capacity. With the necessary qualifications, representatives of this view are Spinoza and his criticism of 'imagination' bound up with history; Lessing, with the famous axiom of his first period, 'The contingent truths of history can never become the proof for the necessary truths of reason'; and Kant, with his view of revelation in history as an illustrated lesson in the truths of reason.

The problems have been with us for a long time. Most of our contemporaries would take it for granted that, apart from the use of reason on which the sciences depend, all knowledge conveyed by the senses is channelled to us through history and that what are supposed to be the eternal truths of metaphysics or ethics are themselves dependent on how we live and the way in which cultures change. The way in which language is necessarily shaped by tradition also makes the absolute autonomy of the subject an illusion: freedom cannot go beyond the transformation of a heritage which one either accepts or rejects.

Be this as it may, when it comes to the question that I have raised, the difficulty seems to persist in other forms. Even if we were to change culture, put reason in its place, and reinstate history, doubts would remain. Does all this make claims that the Absolute has become history any more credible? Can history, withits intrinsic relativity, bear such a weight?

And our hesitations may increase even more. Unless we have a rational conviction of the truth of theism, the whole question of God will come up at this point; it is in this context of historical evidence that we have to ask whether this idea corresponds to a quest for meaning, a pattern of acceptance, within us. Our contemporaries have inherited many puzzles: the frailty of history, which is always open to doubt even if its character is quite different; the charge of imposing an alien law on the most intimate human truths; radical questioning about what is supposed to be the nature of thought about a living Absolute. And none of these can fail to influence a believer concerned about his condition as a witness.

In Pascal, neither the rift between the God of the philosophers and the God of faith nor recourse to human degradation as a way of demonstrating the need for salvation must allow us to forget that we must search for the existential and reflective conditions which are required for an acceptance of the historical revelation that he contrasted with Christian deism. We might doubt the value of his rule of stupefaction, challenge his arguments for supposing that God can only be hidden in the world (inaccessible)

17

or the pointers which allow us to recognize him hidden in Jesus Christ (disguised in order to be discovered). But there can be no question that here he is concerned to have authentic critical verification.

Kierkegaard concedes to Lessing that because historical knowledge lacks certainty and reality, it cannot be the basis for a choice involving eternal happiness. Therefore, he adds, this knowledge contrasts with the only possible point of departure, which is subjectivity, infinite interest. But he argues that it is 'in relation to a historical event' that this 'eternal blessedness of the individual is decided in time'. How can we accept this absolute historical paradox and transcend the 'absurd', avoid 'scandal'? Is the only answer that it is achieved by grace? Or, on the other side of the decision, is it a sheer leap, a radical risk, accepting vertigo poised 'over a depth of seventy thousand feet of water'? Or again, does the feeling of guilt arouse in us a deep thirst for forgiveness?

In fact, Kierkegaard constantly does more than establish existential categories which allow a demonstration of how Christian faith can become ours, step by step. As a philosopher, he also reflects on the relationship between a finite spirit and eternal truth, in order to justify the surprising nature of the message. His meditation moves from life, which is always a contradiction, to a fundamental assessment of the paradox; from the forward movement called for by anything new to the leap of faith; from the 'punctiliar' character of the Absolute to its involvement at that 'point' in history which is the 'instant' of the incarnation; from the fact that God is 'spirit' to his manifestation to humanity in the humble form of the servant. We could hardly be more remote from irrationalism. All the time, the plausibility of the idea of God is never put in doubt, though its context is so often deliberately shifted.

There is a greater shift in Jean Narbert. If our awareness has to strip itself to the point of achieving an 'original affirmation' which makes sense of the idea of the absolute in order to achieve self-understanding, it must also accept its finitude, its inability to attain a total intuitive reflection, its need to look for contingent signs which the Absolute might have given of itself. This adds up to the rehabilitation of history, with the contingency of its moments. Are there lives which bear witness in such a way that they point, whether in experience and history, to someone beyond, lives in which the achievement of freedom and 'transcendence' seem to correspond to their avowed goal? I hesitate over the first of the two aspects of this suggestion, uncertain whether I can involve myself in such an intimate movement, and keep my suppport in reserve.

I feel more at ease when E.Lévinas asks what break-up of thought makes it possible to welcome this word God which is so different that its otherness would seem inevitably to reduce us to silence, and when as an answer he resorts to the old move of the idea of the infinite which cannot be reduced to the act of awareness and contains more than it might seem to. Unease, questioning, desire, expectation, patience eager for something that cannot be grasped – the fragmentation of the more in the less, traces of the infinite in us – could have brought us there. Even more surely, it is in our relationship with others, in our unconditional responsibility towards them, that the circular and self-sufficient totality of our awareness and being falls to pieces, and the infinite points us towards the vulnerable faces of others.

Do we really meet up with history here? This is certainly not a revelation of truth, which in his view would be no more than opinion, perverse heteronomy, myth allied with mysticism in constant opposition to sober reason and prone to fanaticism, an illusion that faith can escape the trap of ontology in which every 'presence' and every 'experience' gets caught. Rather, it is a commandment of revelation which rouses the dulled ethical conscience by a movement coming from outside and creating access to God without alienation.

I find this contrast unsatisfactory. There is such a thing as a biblical 'indicative', the event commemorated by stories and symbolic texts (though far from falling from the skies as ready-made truths, these have to be interpreted). And does not this 'indicative', which marks a turning point, like 'God has delivered (will deliver) his people from Egypt', always precede the 'imperative' in order to prompt action which is free and liberating? Faith is indeed the object of experience, but does it not open itself up by shattering immanence on that of which it has no experience;

19

on that whose presence, always realized through absence, signifies that it is other than being; on that which only reveals itself through witnessing to the extent that an interplay of symbols allows, and is conveyed at a deeper level?

We must be grateful to Paul Ricoeur for having recalled the diversity of forms of writing which make up the Bible – narrative, prophecy, commandments, wisdom discourses, the prayers in the psalms. These far transcend the univocal model of prophetic inspiration and even more rule out both an ethical reductionism and a dangerous abstract and authoritarian interpretation of 'revelation' as external. Ricoeur has also produced what will from now on be a classic analysis of truth as manifestation: the poetic text and the story have a revelatory function which suspends the descriptive and verifiable roles of language and introduces a much more original term of reference, namely that of belonging and being open to a 'world'. Here the previous approaches are broadened and consolidated.

Orientation for a quest

I shall now take up a difficulty I have already raised. Why are we so naive as to conceive of the Absolute, the Infinite, in our image, as a 'person'?

It seems to me that this can hardly be avoided. Could the Absolute have less autonomy and awareness, unimaginable though they might be, than I do? Were I not to imagine the Absolute as personal, could I avoid making him Everything, whereas belief in creation – quite apart from being a religious attitude of thanksgiving for all good and beautiful things – amounts to saying that there is finite being outside him? Do not the very way in which I have expressed the break, and this initiative which goes beyond us, imply that I address Him in personal terms, as I would a close friend, while recognizing that I do not know the true significance of the personal form of address that I use?

There is another point. To speak of God as a Person, an absolute Subject, is to express an experience: the discovery has also constituted me as a unique subject and has opened me up to communication beyond myself. The value and the consistency of my vacillating, ephemeral, changing self, fraught with fantasies and impulses, has been affirmed, so that at the same time I can recognize my solidarity with and responsibility for other people. God does not ground his glory on my non-existence, but if he finds me unfulfilled or wounded, uncertain of my strength, a captive of my egoism or of this boundless joy which is born of sadness, he frees me and restores me, giving me strength in the purest way possible, through a desire to win through.

Perhaps in the end the fact that we address God in a familiar way, in the second person, is the only point of reference around which a sphere can be created and organized in which the essential elements of Christianity can take on meaning and depth. We are well aware that dogma was produced not least as the result of a power struggle and as a consequence of Hellenization. To adopt such a point of reference would be better than to blur the issues with a post-Christian reading of the Bible and the history of the faith, which can only open up horizons, suggest themes, incite to action, leaving open all judgments on reality.

In the same order of ideas, to affirm the absolute self-sufficiency of God might well seem too 'Greek' and not 'biblical' enough – but it is perhaps unwise to suggest that God is only fulfilled through what he brings about in us. Similarly, it is probably naive to stress his unconditional omnipotence and omniscience, in the face of so many difficulties, but all things considered, it is somewhat frivolous to deny the capacity for 'announcing what is to come' and 'realizing the desires of the heart' which led Israel from belief in the saving power of deity to faith in the creative gift of the one true God. The pathos of the weak God replacing the fanfares of the celestial monarch: we always want to say more than we know.

I have said that God is not everything. So being and goodness exist. Moreover, if I understand rightly, he does not ask me to turn away from things or from a dimension of myself to find him. He is not of the order of what he creates, nor does he expect people to 'prefer' him. He expects them to love him alone with an absolute love. He is not jealous of my human happiness but rather takes delight in the greatness of his creatures. I shall have to return later to the consequences that I should draw from this twofold affirmation, in my life as a Christian and in my understanding of witnessing.

As to the word 'God' which I have used, does it not in fact sum up all the problems? There is the equivocation of providentialist deism which absorbed faith and which for two centuries has been dead and buried along with Dame Metaphysics, its partner; the burdensome heritage of the social and psychological functions of 'God' in Christianity; and above all the emptiness or the vagueness of a concept which bolsters the illusion that people who use it know what they are talking about.

Since we complain about the esoteric character of our Christian vocabulary, would it not be strange if we gave up the one word the import of which everyone understands? People know that 'God' denotes the quest for or an affirmation of the Absolute. It is utterly indeterminate, and in a way must remain so, given our lack of knowledge. Our task is to define it as far as we can, not by giving it a 'meaning' but by defining the One to whom it refers through our very attitude towards him, which language will reveal. So it is important that this word should always appear as a personal name (without an article) and should indicate a relationship (my God, our God).

I might also ask what other term we should use. The more rarefied and striking the metaphors we employ, the more tired they become; the great abstract words are deceptive, producing more illusion. And we know full well the abuse of language which has led to the rhetoric of the Wholly Other, if only to indicate, in full awareness of the circumstances, a radical break with the One who is neither the object nor the subject of words – the One who is accessible most specifically through ecstasy, or through communion with the intermediate realities which lead to him, or again through participation by virtue of the discovery of unity within ourselves.

But is not God named in the Bible? Leaving aside the tetragrammaton YHWH – for after three thousand years we still do not know whether it denotes an end of not-receiving, a future of promise or a basis for the Greek ontologies to come – has he not revealed himself as Father? Indeed. The transition from the 'God of the Fathers' to 'God our Father' in the teaching of Jesus marks an important shift within the Jewish tradition to the degree that it stresses proximity, mercy, tender care. At the same time, because this is a personal name it does not get beyond the level of metaphor, the parable of the prodigal son. And a good thing too! The social and psychological functions of the divine Fatherhood were so burdensome that we are aware of the danger of building up a whole spiritual life on this conception. Attempts are being made to compensate for the way in which God is traditionally portrayed as masculine – which is in any case relative, to the extent that this 'father' figure performs roles which are associated with the mother. However, the image of the primeval mother is so much more perilous than that of the ideal and immortal father that it would be much better to suppress them both. So let us be content with making gentle use of 'Our Father who art in heaven', a clause in which the second phrase destroys the illusion that the first gives a quasi-definition of 'God'.

I have not forgotten that stress on the connotations of a particular form of behaviour or portrayal – including the overtones to the very sensitive matter of the practice of intercession to Mary – will always lead to divisions among believers. There will be those who cannot or will not see clearly; those who, at the time of a new critical advance, will be impatient to get going towards a purer view of the faith; and those who think that everything is ambiguous and that no religious form is real unless it expresses a human sentiment, that it provides an important extra dimension, not so much in itself as in the effective part it plays in our emotional life – whether neutral, beneficial or toxic.

It will be argued that people speak in an infinitely more personal sense of the 'Father' of the 'Son' who is Jesus Christ. When we use these words, and also talk of the 'Spirit', do we not come near to the communication of the Name that cannot be known? My reply would take the form of two further questions. If we were not concerned with imagery, would it not do just as well to describe this unique relationship by saing that he is the X of this Y? Were not the three terms God (the Father), the Son of God (Jesus, designated by a late Hellenistic title, expressing the full awareness of his mystery attained gradually through the 'resurrection'), and the Spirit of God (inspiration, both hidden and with clearly visible effects) used to help us to understand the reality and the evocativeness of the manifestation of God in the human destiny of Jesus and his presence in our hearts after the 'departure' of Christ, while preserving his absolute transcendence? And in doing so did they not remain within the realm of metaphor?

Meanwhile a second shift had come about, as a result of which the New Testament came into being: if God has made himself visible at this point and if he has thus opened himself to the inner hearts of believers, it is because he is himself gift, Love. Was this more than to affirm a tendency in him to love us, undeniable but incomprehensible and too often disconcerting? Was this the Name of the Father? Was it also necessary for the word God, which had hitherto been reserved for him, soon to be extended to include what were later called the three 'persons'? Was the dogma – and the third displacement – of the eternal communion of the Three really needed to express the reality of the historical commitment of God in respect of his otherness? Whatever the answers, this is how history was made.

Choosing a language

We must take up the threads again. We were talking about the condition of the witness. Then there was the other person, facing him, whom we imagine questioning him and being interested in the resources by which he lives; someone who has the capacity to understand, if not to accept. And then there is the matter of God. My question here is not what should be talked about first, nor what the starting point for it is, but the kind of conversation we might have nowadays in which we wanted to use the word God.

Witnessing to God gradually makes its mark on language through imagery, through a move made by the witness or through a trace left in him or her. (Some of them will not so much be described by the person doing the talking as discovered by his conversation partner in his life-style or the way in which he expresses himself.) Witnessing makes its mark through the story of an experience or the evocation of a way of living, through a

24

basic reflection on the possibility of knowing God, and finally through a quite distinctive vocabulary – that related to the coming of his 'kingdom' – which cries out not only to be explained but more radically to be interpreted.

In our day, I do not have much trust in the evocative power of the great metaphors taken from human life or from the cosmos with due correction – poetry, too, had its negative theology – to put the stamp of mystery on them. No matter whether this imagery comes from the countryside, from love, from the stars, or makes use of the four elements; no matter whether it comes from the rock to the spring or from the wind to the flame, its power has been overworked. Above all, it brushes aside too readily our shame, our doubts, our need to be reassured.

A blank space in the text, a patch of silence, a sudden pause while talking ought to be the first introduction of God into speech or writing. A manoeuvre to gain attention? No, a real confession of our permanent ineptitude.

Empty space has a decisive role in Chinese painting, and re-reading these lines makes me think of it. It also suggests another comparison: the perspective in the countrysides painted by the Song masters is organized around an invisible point of reference. A series of rocks, twisted trees, a ship are orientated on it; our attention is drawn in a different direction from the obvious one, that of the light. Though absent from the page or the spoken phrase, God draws the whole of it towards himself.

The believer must be seen as a man, a woman, before a threshold – a door, a window, a low wall, a grille, a parapet; or on a frontier, a boundary, a col, a fence, the edge of a desert, the shore of a sea; as a man, a woman, watching, on guard, constantly waiting. This threshold position is not a complete expression of our witnessing: we should also try to name that which never ceases to come. Nor is it specific; others than believers reach out beyond themselves in this way. However, this position is the only one which bears witness in its supreme truth: that which is distant, hoped-for, is always to come, always transcends the signs of its coming.

What was revelatory about Jesus to a supreme degree, what we have been given to testify to as witnesses, is a way of orientating our being on God, acting as characters to inscribe him on that movement which points towards him without being able to show him. It is one way of remaining before him, with him, a way which is so deep down within us that while sometimes it may be expressed, more often it has to be guessed at.

Up to a certain point my own love for God *is* the witness that I make to him. It is meaningful in human terms, because while there will be some who see it as alienation, others can find there the supreme creation possible; it is ambiguous, since the witness has only been given properly if it is recognized as the sap and not the fruit. To tell the truth, this love is often the only indication which remains to me of His passing, along with the memory of the hours when I have seemed to feel it growing in me.

Because it isolates the essential feature, that aspect which cannot be confused with anything else, the statement I have just made is certainly too restrained: the trace, the observable imprint of God in a life, goes beyond any deliberate action we make to put ourselves in touch with him. The attitude of Jesus towards those whom he meets is already an eloquent sign of the One to whom he bears witness: I have changed, since the irruption of God in me and as a result of that irruption, and others have been changed even more.

However, the mark of such a change still retains the twofold ambiguity which affects every sign. First there is the ambiguity which derives from its origin: not only can it be derived, like all forms of conduct, including religious ones, from a personal or cultural history; even the search for it is, as I have said, a hazardous matter, because this mark has no specific character. Then there is the ambiguity which arises from different, not to say opposed, interpretations of the faith: change and change about there will be a preference for the 'unusual', or for something else, the miracle or the incandescence of the ordinary, detachment or involvement, incarnation or escape.

If the believer actually comes to the point of speaking of his experience, describing it, he will say that it is in some ways paradoxical. Confessing that he finds himself abandoned, dispossessed, at the very point of hearing a word of authentic revelation and receiving an inestimable gift, he will continue to preserve the absolute mystery of the Other, though this has made him a witness by manifestation.

This experience, then, takes many forms, but its most valuable contribution consists in giving a kind of unity to life - a bridge built between the realms of a broken existence rather than a 'balcony on the world' – which only emerges if it is in accord with the common source of nature and history. Or, if the believer is not only seen to be standing expectantly on a threshold, but actually feels that he is standing there, the invisible line which links him with the unknown yet separates him from it does not mark off 'another world', since it pervades all his thought, his action, his emotions, his encounters.

This paradoxical language will leave its mark on all reflection about possible relationship with God: as I have said, one will never speak of presence without evoking the absence which makes that presence so disconcerting and yet does not negate it. At all times discussion of knowledge has dealt with ignorance, since in the Bible itself, from one end to another, anthropomorphism associated with a deep awareness of the holiness and freedom of God has allowed a combination of God's transcendence and nearness, our difference from him and our creaturely resemblance to him.

Above all, for believers in our century, the certainty of faith in God can only be affirmed in its uncertainty: not as parts in doubtful balance, but as the radical components of experience - one existential and the other rational. This must happen to the point when the action of God in us and our own action are both seen to be at work, no longer as forces allied in a dynamic of 'grace', but by the very mystery of 'creation' which is always present to us and by the renewing power of the discovery of an absolute love which draws us on.

That is the subject-matter of the old theme of the reign or kingdom of God. That kingdom is the essential element, first, in the teaching and the hope of Jesus, and then in the desire of the disciples as they look for his 'return' in glory – whether or not they use the word. It is near, very near – we already seem to be able to touch it, though then it eludes our grasp and can only be possessed after a formidable crisis.

27

This kingdom appears as something which is both in the future and yet anticipated, indeed inaugurated, in the action and even the person of Jesus: it is imminent and yet so unforeseeable that no one knows its date; it is as simple as life and as unimaginable as God's 'heaven'; it is earthly to the point of bringing a cure for every ill with the overturning of unjust social situations and as definitive as the resurrection. It calls for an ardent and tense vigil, or patient waiting down the long days.

The intrinsic paradox of our experience is not the only reason for the oscillation of these formulas; the communities which are responsible for handing them down to us have already introduced into them, by their interpretations, an ambiguity which has remained ever since. In immediate terms their hope in fact proved deceptive, and to avoid the conclusion that the message was mere imposture or illusion, they had to interpret it in lives to which only death put an end and in a history which did not seem to want to stop.

We cannot disguise the fact that there have been many interpretations of the expectation of the kingdom. So if we want to understand what has become of this old way of speaking of God while keeping intact a respect for his mystery – in that respect rather like the 'divine passive': 'they will be comforted', meaning, 'someone will comfort them' – we are led both to ask about the ultimate significance of Christian witness for human life and to discover the need to make choices. The historical current which issued from Jesus is too complex and too full of contrast for anyone involved in it not to be forced to state, with clarity, at the risk of a conflict, the version on which he takes his stand.

3

The basic interpretation of Christian witness

Flight from the world

The marvellous kingdom which God is expected to inaugurate through an imminent decisive action interrupts everything by the urgency of its coming. In the life-style of Jesus and the first Christians, several dimensions of everyday life are as it were suspended or relatively ignored: the preservation of the political or social *status quo*, even though it may be seen to be unjust; the lack of time for marriage, or the view that there is no point in it, even though it is recognized as being fundamentally good.

To speak only in terms of the second collapse of short-term hope, the one experienced by the disciples after the 'departure' of Jesus: inevitably there had to emerge imperceptibly out of this disappointment a new reading which provided a long-term interpretation of the guidelines that he had given, in which the last things tended to become more and more an embellishment. The way in which he had taught and acted in inaugurating the kingdom in the present-day experience of this world provided a basis for this reinterpretation.

Traces of it are present everywhere in the books of the New Testament: for Luke the kingdom is realized in the form of the church, and the eschatological crisis takes place in the cross of everyday life; for John it comes about in the experience of the faith and love of the community. Paul had to revise his ideas of marriage (from remedy to mystery) and of death (from assumption to being snatched away, in order to go to live 'with the Lord'). But these

29

are never more than incomplete sketches, often emended by others with more old-fashioned views, and the shift – from ecstasy to inscription – always remains partial.

That is why one can choose to limit the shift as far as possible, perhaps by suggesting that a decisive event could still take place, but above all by planning to keep the *suspense* and to reduce to a minimum the element which affects our present life. Very soon the aspiration to martyrdom and then flight to the desert as a substitute for persecution came to embody this option in an extreme way – in both cases out of a desire to face up to the ultimate crisis by fighting against the powers of evil.

Subsequently, 'monastic' Christianity, in the sense of a universal model or an ideology laying claim to all Christianity, albeit in a nostalgic or hesitant way, has remained one of the possible poles in an interpretation of the Origin. That is one way of understanding monasticism – certainly not the only one, but it is difficult for the 'religious life' to be free of it - which becomes an overall vision of Christian existence.

Living apart, escaping the world, is a 'separation', a literal break, which is quite different from the one achieved at the heart of presence and communion by a rejection of inauthenticity and egoism. Here there is a use of the word 'world' which tends to confuse such different elements as the whole material creation, the human species, the maleficent social network created by injustice and superficiality, the culture fashioned by human beings who fill it with their discoveries and embody their values in it.

This 'world' appears to be an ethical obstacle to human salvation: an obsession with sin entails the need to hold corrupt nature in check; hence universal pessimism, the primacy of asceticism, and soon of dolorism. Sometimes 'the world' is even understood as a hindrance to humanity; it is mistrust of the body, a quest for an absence of feeling through the extinction of the passions, the attraction of an 'angelic life', pure contemplation, a paradise rediscovered outside the secular sphere. The discourse of the spiritual masters is dominated by the polarity of the heavenly and the earthly, the spiritual and the carnal, the invisible and the visible, the eternal and the transitory, the intelligible and the sensible, just as in secular life this polarity calls for the subordination of the temporal.

In a way quite alien to biblical faith, one or the other gave rise to a profound mistrust of pleasure, an enormous sense of guilt, and a veritable obsession with sex. One might argue that this obsession has been the moral neurosis of Christianity and its most evident denial of the human. So many laws made by the ecclesiastical authorities, which are still in force, derive from this aberrant attitude, as, paradoxically, do more than one notion dear to the heart of very open Christians. This is evidence of an absolutizing of sexuality, a kind of all-or-nothing, which is perhaps just one more aspect of this mistrust and contempt.

It must, of course, be recognized that for the most part this monastic complex is related to a current of unitive mysticism originating in Neoplatonism which has proved both important and seductive. It runs through the three monotheistic religions and closely links the desire to be united to the divine Essence with the demand to strip oneself of everything to the point of self-annihilation. It corresponds to several deep aspirations of every believer – even if it owes its success even more to the resolution it offers of our earliest fantasies of fusion, those which are most repressed in institutional religion, while avoiding the terror of a dissolution of the self. However, it only teaches us how to find freedom and how to pray silently and continuously if we accept its twofold derivation, which is both excessive and deadly. One might doubt whether it is in the mainstream of the prophets, the Psalmists and Jesus.

Beyond question, no one nowadays would dream of offering an out-and-out defence of these versions of Christianity. However, deeply rooted doubts remain, and that means that they cannot be dismissed with a clear conscience. Might not these alone be authentic religion, and all the rest superficiality, incoherence, mediocre compromise? This hesitation, sometimes amounting to fascination, leaves its stamp on the judgments, the admiration, the thoughtless impulses of so many believers and indeed unbelievers. A backlash from it is inevitable, regardless of whether such impulses are soon forgotten or whether they serve as a spur to action.

If we are to grasp the essential religious force of the 'monastic' interpretation – which to a greater or lesser degree prolongs the original suspense by touching the human realm, the earth, just with the finger tips – and also the disquiet that it sometimes awakens in us, beyond question we need to get back to the initial moment of every conversion, which is a rediscovery of the characteristics of the historic beginnings of the faith: God occupies the whole field of consciousness, he seems to be everything; it is as though he were utterly sufficient. So there is inevitably a monastic moment in which the 'absolute ideal of the cloister' comes to birth in every individual; and this later produces nostalgia for what has been 'lost' or 'missed'. However, the only morrow promised to this sudden flash is that promised to passionate love, i.e death; the dimension of time, and therefore of life, is alien to it.

We can understand that from such a perspective the witnessing which calls for attention or provides the evidence is the literal, naked witness offered to the Absolute. The transparency, as people love to say, of the believer, the 'sacrifice' offered of his or her earthly life, and sometimes the wonders of the sacred which shine out in our disasters, will be the authentic ways to the discovery of God. The less human, the more divine: the truest witness is the 'trappist' (or the yogi) of one's dreams, the one whom one transposes, by the virtue of 'detachment', to the heart of secular existence.

The incarnation

Thus a good deal is at stake in this question, which remains uncertain by virtue of its original ambiguity. What place is to be given to earthly human life – the body, sexuality, work, relationships, political responsibility, intellectual activity and the spiritual experience of the beauty of nature or art – in faith and in the relationship to God that this sets in motion? Is the option of turning aside from the world to find Him the only one? Is the maximum of Christianity achieved only by means of an excessive detachment? Do I really have to reduce to silence this stubbornness, this obstinate protest made with all my being, that I should not be asked to deny or mutilate my humanity in order to approach God, for whom I am seized with so great a desire?

The suspense born of imminence has hidden from us a much more profound constant in the biblical tradition. We have to see in the prophets of Israel the passion of God for the life of his people: for its carnal, everyday existence, for its collective destiny, for its social customs – the demand for justice, the promise of happiness – with a growing awareness of the universality of his designs for humanity.

The creation stories tell us the same thing: a radical *yes* to the goodness of life – so good that God marvels at it – a blessing on human existence, sexuality, work, that no fault can entirely abolish. For this *yes* is a yes now: by universalizing it, the creation story describes the present experience of the divine covenant offered to humanity despite our evasion and our hardness of heart.

The proclamation of the kingdom of God at the centre of the preaching of Jesus is concerned with every aspect of the personal life of women and men. If it anticipates that kingdom, it does so by acts of compassion for earthly ills, by the transgression of established norms which in fact inaugurate another kind of society. A filial awareness of God is inseparable from these practices: in the message, promises and demands go hand in hand.

That is why, I ought to say in passing, I am glad to be a Christian: the words and actions of Jesus – at least those told of him, and those traces are enough for me – are expressions and realizations of attitudes that I love, on which I want to base my life. I am persuaded that they arouse delight at the depths of our being, far more than their opposites which make our heart beat more strongly. Brotherhood, gentleness, service, forgiveness, contagious peace, the purity of a tranquil heart, a concern for human dignity and justice, seem to me to represent the better things of this earth – provided that they are not based on the fear of pleasure and the rechannelling of aggression.

At the heart of this complex of attitudes we find what has made Jesus of Nazareth an unforgettable figure: unconditional welcome, compassion for all distress, forgiveness for all failings,

33

the reinstatement of the 'impure' in the community, the acceptance of the other as he or she is, no matter what. Here we find
pity – an admirable word, degraded by condescension, rejected
by wounded pride; but it is a word which expresses total understanding, total solidarity with the suffering of our kin. Here is
welcome: all the nobility of someone standing on his doorstep,
receiving the stranger, introducing him into his house, for ever
fixed in that gesture which is the beginning of our humanity – the
metaphor for so many encounters where a word has meant
welcome and where for lack of a word we have missed the
opportunity for ever. Here is hope for others: no matter how shut
in, no matter how overwhelmed a person may be, a spark of
freedom, of love, of beauty can still be born of him or her. Here
is obstinate good will, hope without illusion, which goes beyond
the contortions of psychology to the depths of the being whom
God seeks and calls; sometimes a creative avowal of what he or
she looks for beyond expectation, in spite of everything.

At the heart of this heart, dearer to me than anything else, is
this habit of Jesus of going to the roots of the situations that he
discovers, rejecting all formalism, even at its most noble, and
combining in his subversive way the distinctive truth of a human
situation and a relationship to God. Here is the giddy responsibility of evaluating my own life without false pretences or infallible
criteria, the impossibility of making myself the judge of others.

Finally, what could be the meaning of the Christian re-reading
of the history of Jesus in the light of the experience of his risen
glory, as 'incarnation', if not to affirm that God, taking the risk of
history and humanity, has manifested himself in contingent
existence: the time, the place made decisive, the countenance
seen as that of God, the suffering capable of changing significance?
The authenticity and integrity of this human condition will always
be recalled in the face of every kind of gnosticism: 'That which is
not assumed is not saved.'

I spoke of 'the countenance seen as that of God'. The 'little one',
the stranger whom I recognize as my neighbour because he calls
me, the one through whom I welcome Jesus and finally the One
who has sent him (by receiving him, feeding him, clothing him,
visiting him) – with what mystery will he not veil himself once

his face is made the human manifestation of God towards us? The image has become an icon, the other leads me to God and God leads me to the other, when I love Him and pray to Him. Where would I have known Him other than in his advent, drawing me into the movement of his pity, his incarnation?

So another logic, the opposite to the flight from the world, and more original, appears, in order to remove the constant hesitation. Here there is an emphasis on a reinterpretation in terms of existence and history. They are the context in which the waiting takes place; it is in my bodily life, my spiritual life, my future in this world, that there is a welcome for the kingdom. It is to discover the maximum for humanity that I seek the maximum for God. In a similar way, the 'monastic' moment of conversion, saturated by a kind of divine immediacy, must be matched by a second moment that might be called 'humanist', reintegrating this intuition of the Absolute into the reality of a history without losing the transcendent reference.

The eschatological verve of Christianity – the expectation of the ultimate – is itself preserved by the substitution of enforced, mutilating suspense with a patient, peaceful vigilance, when the imminent coming of the kingdom becomes incessant, when tension is succeeded by attention. We find that this distance which is unbridgeable (though we are promised that we shall overcome it), this future void which calls us and compels us to go on, is already there. or infinitely close and always keeping its distance.

An integrally human Christianity

In this perspective, the significance of witness also changes: witnessing to the Absolute in his creative love and his incarnation substitutes density for transparency, and makes its offering of the heart regardless of whether the hands are full or empty, without sacrificing anything to give glory to God. If the word of Another is to be heard in that of the believer, if a presence makes itself felt in his existence – and this word and this presence may be less brilliant but nevertheless evocative of the One who does not manifest himself by humiliating his creature – it is certainly

35

through their poverty, their avowed weakness in speaking of God, in presenting God; but it is also through their human quality, their human authenticity, their refusal to trifle with the chances and the risks of our condition.

This choice, which has to be made, can be made in more or less radical ways. Intrinsically it calls for as complete an assessment as possible of the positive experiences or values, the challenges which make up the life of a man or a woman. The elemental features of personal existence and the complexity of collective existence do not estrange people from God but can be intermediaries in the quest for him, even if that quest transcends them all and is fulfilled in an original activity, prayer – though that is, of course, a spiritual human activity.

That is why from the start of any reflection on faith and witness it would be wise to avoid a binary contrast between the 'Christian' and the 'human being' which the subsequent course of the discussion did not transcend. Ultimately, 'Christian' is never more than an adjective: it is applied to one and the same integral human subject who, on becoming a believer, can be considered and named from the perspective of faith. It is not that being human and being a Christian are purely and simply identical: there are aspects of Christian experience which at particular moments go beyond what humanity understands by living, which is historical, and even go beyond every intrinsic possibility of our species. However, these aspects are realized in human beings, so human beings must be capable of them – and that includes the unique achievement, unprecedented for a man, of being Son of God!

To develop the point in a more dynamic way, I would be ready to argue that no advance is possible in the life of faith and in our understanding of it which is not based on a growth of human maturity within us. And the reverse is no less true – as a general rule, since one knows very poor or almost derelict human beings who have borne admirable fruits of the gospel, and authentic believers who have felt that they have to unburden themselves to the point of exhaustion. I want to speak here not only of existential depth but also of emotional development – as allowed by the ups and downs of our life or as helped by psychotherapeutic treatment – while knowing that sometimes it will sweep away or at least dislodge a faith which is too entangled in the infantile bonds of our personality.

I have spoken of risks and challenges. So this is no apologia (whether puerile or derogatory) for 'fulfilment', but a whole-hearted assent to the mixed reality which is human life. Before helping us to face its dilemmas, the gospel calls us to accomplish its possibilities – and sometimes it is necessary to believe in order for them to arise.

That is one of the aspects of my witnessing. We only begin to discover the greatness of God when we understand that the greatness of man does not put it in the shade: only petty thoughts can make him a cruel master or jealous of what he has made. And we only progress in this initiation when we awaken to the immensity and the complexity of the universe, to the variety of faces shown by God to those men and women whose every quest, every creation, teaches the believer something of him.

As to the other aspect: in other books I have stressed to such a degree the difficult hope raised by faith in the face of evil, misfortune, the infinite misery of life, that I need not return to that question here. Since everyone knows that the only fitting attitude to evil is to fight against it, talking and above all theorizing about it as little as possible, it will be enough to say once again that the keywords which are used below in a positive sense conceal another, more obscure but very precious, insight into this side of existence.

The 'incarnation' also means that through the hands of Jesus God has not only touched all the joys of life – fresh mornings, the joys of marriage, good friendships, the warmth of home – but, nailed to the cross, the depths of misery: there, in the darkness, something has changed. 'Creation' again signifies that if there is in God the memory of the slightest spark of goodness or the most fleeting trace of beauty, this faithful concern has the unimaginable capacity to make those men and women whom he loves and remembers live for ever. Finally, the 'greatness' of God implies that if I am right not to see myself guilty of exaggerating evil and ceaselessly questioning my God, as a corollary I must understand

and accept that He is boundless, incomprehensible wisdom, and in confessing this find my peace.

I am not denying moral evil, failure, wrongdoing, sin. I am simply saying that it is absurd to claim that the whole of humanity is completely steeped in it to the point of not being able to perform the smallest act of true goodness, for the undeniable but irrelevant reason that only God can take the initiative in introducing us into his friendship. It is absurd to seek the source of all our evils in our mistakes; and to rely our feelings of guilt, which, while infinitely real, more often than not have nothing to do with our ethical life, in order to procure for ourselves evidence of our secret need of divine help.

Beyond question human beings are better than they are said to be; they are also worse, for the 'saints' still have a great many weaknesses and a great many attitudes that they would judge to be evil, were these weaknesses and attitudes transposed to a context in which they could recognize them. Without any doubt it is their law which all too often, as Paul said, creates sin by making an issue of it – the fascination of the transgression and above all the aberrant indictment of someone who, without such legalistic statements, would be innocent – and by imprisoning people in it. Faith breaks open the barriers and introduces forgiveness and the intimate strength of love: as I have said, it affirms my own self.

How? Not as a psychotherapist would do it, getting my innermost being back to work again – that is our business, to be done with the means at our disposal. But if the bankruptcy of an emotional investment – through bereavement or loss of work – can make a personality disintegrate, conversely a positive motivation, of the order of love and meaning, can make it whole, unite it and even, if the person is young, contribute towards structuring it.

The word freedom, sometimes a slogan of Christians and sometimes the great fear of their leaders and a rallying point for their opponents, presents itself as a designation of both these aspects together. This freedom is freedom – as one can admit without hesitation – by virtue of the knowledge of supreme joy, within a limited horizon; it is freedom from those bonds which are so reluctant to let us go; freedom of loving and freedom to love. It is freedom – and here is something we may be more ready to forget – from all law, in order to give free play to a loving, creative spontaneity, an impulse of the Spirit reaching to our innermost depths, a response accorded to man who is the 'image of God' by virtue of this very freedom.

Such an internalization of the principles of human conduct – aimed at putting them into practice effectively! – should have made it possible to welcome the claim to autonomy which since the Renaissance and above all since the eighteenth century has represented a decisive step by humanity on the way towards its adulthood rather than interpreting it as a revolt against God, even if it was inevitably accompanied by a liberation from direct religious controls and therefore from subordination to ecclesiastical powers. Autonomy is not autarky, a self-sufficient closed society, and at the same time human beings can also remain open to transcendence. Is the fact that this autonomy has so often been taken away the cause or effect of the sterile hardening of the churches?

This autonomy should also have guaranteed the basic principle of any community which emerges from the gospel: the freedom of the Christian in the church, a freedom that no one has the right to take away. It should have meant fewer laws, with those that remained being educative or provisional; an egalitarian simplicity among communities whose powers (and all human groups have to have powers) would be slight and understood as the modest expression of fellowship between adult, enlightened believers, enjoying free access to their God. It should have meant inalienable rights of belonging, self-expression and discernment, with each individual and each community in turn accepting the right to be challenged by the free word of others.

An essential point still has to be made. The choice of human integrity as a criterion of authenticity, the choice of freedom as a test of whether the gospel has been put into practice, calls for humanization and liberation where these things are missing. The Christian must feel called to denounce every situation of underdevelopment, alienation or oppression – whether personal or communal – in the name of his faith, and in such contexts any reference to spiritual growth, poverty of the heart and inner freedom (which in fact can arise from anywhere, at any time) smacks of imposture.

Questions of vocabulary

I have sketched out a critique of the 'monastic' ideology – is 'the religious life' included? Yes, if it is defined as universal renunciation, objectively superior because it establishes a 'direct' link with the kingdom of God, or even just radical in its abolition of inalienable dimensions of human life like sexuality, economic responsibility, control of one's own existence.

That would be a delusion. Nowadays we cannot fail to sense our mixed motives, those secret pressures which sometimes come to uplift us and sometimes to destroy us. Moreover, it would be an impossibility: such fundamental realities can only be disguised and displaced, not overcome. And it would be an error of judgment: every human being evolves, especially in his or her emotional life. We mature and risk finding ourselves different people: 'There is no migration beyond the bounds of humanity.'

In connection with the analysis that I have already embarked on, I would say that religious life can be defended only as a way of reintegration into the specific features of existence, a way of living them out – starting from the initial immediate and radical commitment of faith – not as a way of by-passing them. This way of living is marked by partial renunciations: voluntary impoverishment, with effective economic responsibility based on the gospel criteria of freedom and sharing; obedience as an exercise in the responsible orientation of one's existence within a dialogue among the community; celibacy and chastity as part of an awareness of emotion, to the degree accepted within the group and with scrupulous attention to others whose infantile and irrepressible sexuality or disguised emotiveness sometimes cheapens them.

Such a way of life, which is not specific to Christianity, can be chosen with a view either to religious experience or to service in the gospel, because many people think that conditions favour it. There would be scope, beyond these criteria of acceptability, for testing the arguments and evaluating the successes and drawbacks, both collective and personal. I have come across fine examples of its having been put into practice, above all in religious life among women, and historians have long been aware of the extraordinary creativity of monastic humanism.

Christian life has its times of necessary asceticism and no less indispensable positive human advancement, both of which are needed for its growth. Consequently we might ask whether the most penetrating question to raise about religious life – since it purports to offer everyone the opportunity for a personal spiritual journey – is not: What is the invariable maximum demanded of those who want to become involved, and how confident can one be that renunciation alone will see one through? The way to the fulfilment of the gospel is long, full of detours, and different for each individual; sometimes progress depends on freedom to deprive oneself (freedom from bondage) and sometimes it depends on freedom to indulge oneself (freedom from prohibitions). Can this alternation or succession be integrated into an institution or must it lead to our supposing such an institution to be temporary? But in that case, who ensures its continuity?

There is another question. Why have I not spoken of 'Christian humanism'? I have not done so, in order to spare myself being involved in excessively complicated debates: the optimism of the humanists of the Reformation and Luther's criticism; the excesses of the idealist stage in the nineteenth century; the Marxist challenge to the cultural code of the commercial and industrial middle classes which did not humanize real social relationships: the confrontation of humanisms with the shattering of their vision of man and civilization. All that prompts modesty and reserve in the use of this terminology.

If I speak, cautiously, of an 'authentically' human Christianity, the expression seems to me feeble. If I use the adjective 'integral', I have to make it quite clear – in contrast to the famous attempt by Jacques Maritain – that the issue here is not to summon humanity to examine and fulfil itself, through institutions and through reflections, thanks to Christianity; the situation is quite the reverse: Christian existence is in turn under pressure not to avoid anything human.

If I were to conjure up a 'humanist' Christianity, to enliven my argument and provide a contrast with the adjective 'monastic', it would have to be distinguished from the one-dimensional and blissfully optimistic ideology of secularization, which has recently been created with a view to justifying the West in the full flood of expansion. For such a Christianity the Christian who conforms with the 'divine plan' is one who is laicized or (translated into ethical terms) freed from the 'religious' dimension, to the degree of disappearing into the human dough which proves quite easy to leaven.

In reality the unity of life according to the gospel presents itself to us as an experience to which there are two approaches, coherent but not monistic: to work for humanity is not to pray, and to pray is not to act. There is a satisfying but unstable balance which is always on the very point of being disturbed, of being impoverished, of imperceptibly deflecting the energy invested in it. There will always be a need for thoughts, words, times to incarnate both historical achievement and the excesses of the dialogue of faith.

One of the equivocal factors in the present situation is the blossoming of neo-conservative movements which have every appearance of modernity in their contemporary style, their knowledge of techniques and publicity, and above all in their integration of a large range of secular life into the full reality of a doctrinaire, authoritarian, supernaturalist view of things. They embody the secret option of a broader current which tends to permeate the whole church.

Their basic postulate is unity of personality through faith in Jesus Christ. One cannot deny that this unifying power is one of the essential aspects of the experience of a believer, presupposing or reinforcing in us a consistent selfhood without failing to recognize the illusions of the possibility of a clear conscience and without accepting the nihilism of a self which has been irremediably shattered. But this unity can be understood in various ways. It can be seen in monastic terms: God is everything (in himself), so he must become everything for me. Or again, it can be understood in humanistic terms. There is good outside this God and yet He does not compete with things: the loftiest vision is realized through constant intermediaries, and unity comes about through the acceptance of plurality.

The neo-conservative spiritualities move from the unity offered by faith to a Christian identity which is thought to be quite specific and handed down from on high: for example, they have a Christian ethic capable of decreeing that a particular way of behaving is objectively, invariably, good or bad. It is easy enough to see where this will lead – as well as where it will not: to a one-track view of the church, with a hierarchical and centralist doctrine of authority, and a uniform type of politics, albeit of a democratic kind.

And all that makes up the church. Am I also to be a witness to such a mixed reality?

Witnessing and the church

Witnessing comes about in a community and has its roots there; in turn, it points back there. We also bear witness to our church; we are not fully ourselves unless we, too, at certain moments, become part of the community.

That is possible. There are always witnesses and communities in the historical, empirical churches. In reality these witnesses and these communities are the 'church'.

If I bear witness, it is in the name of the good news which tends to spread of its own accord, in the name of my faith which I offer back to God in praise, and because this is the essential responsibility of all Christians. Thus we are 'sent' by God himself, prior to any mission of the church; and our witness is egalitarian, 'ordination' being relative to the communities and to their communion, and not to witnessing.

The interplay between 'I' and 'we' which characterizes witness must be taken up on a larger scale: that of the relationship between a particular community – though the church is entirely present in it – and the church of all times and all places which alone hands down all the experience, all the riches which its diversity allows to the bold and which its long history relativizes. Because the church is a social reality living in history, it has to have an identity; it seems to me that this is provided above all by the eucharist: the remembrance of its beginnings, an action which says all that needs to be said. The church also has to be able to recognize itself

43

in a profession of faith of which the essential, original nucleus, indicating *in whom* it believes, is more important than the burgeoning additions, and the basic continuity is more important than the successive forms of expression. Finally, the church needs ministries – to direct and unify it – the contingent forms of which should preoccupy it less than the evangelical style of their functioning.

What more need I say? That is the church which is essential to my witnessing, the church to which I can bear witness. Is the rest, while not to be scorned, really so important? At most, I might go on to formulate some rules from this wisdom, acquired not without pain, which allow me to live my life with serenity.

It seems to me that the essential thing is to devote one's energies only to basic Christian existence – that workshop whose grey windows can be transformed into luminous stained glass. My existence is that of the beings for whom I am concerned, using my strength to help them to develop where this is what is called for, where this is possible. I have neither charge nor care of the wider groupings, of the days after tomorrow.

Beyond question it is right that some people should become more involved in institutional struggles – in the hope either of making modest advances or of guaranteeing more freedom for others. It is also right that I should lend them my support. But it is more than an error, it is perhaps a basic fault, to devote one's passions and one's faith to such a struggle.

My security in the church and a kind of indifference to what people might think or do about me is rooted in my certainty of belonging originally, inalienably, to it by my faith and my baptism. The son is at home in his own house.

On the other hand, I cannot imagine a critical freedom which could be exercised with sensationalism or ill-humour, in opposition to what we have learned of the life of the Spirit: seriousness, modesty. I cannot conceive of it without love.

It is true that love can be deceived. But it would be preferable not to surrender oneself to ill-feeling. To lose the capacity to see and to speak of the greatness and beauty of the church – both that which is made manifest and that which still remains anonymous and hidden – simply because someone has tried to pull the wool over our eyes or because our eyesight has become more acute would be to fall into the opposite trap.

An important thing about witnessing is that I should not hold myself responsible for follies and crimes past and present, even if this goes against the unconditional positions for and against. Solidarity, which one cannot reject, does not go beyond accepting the consequences of all these blunders.

We need to evaluate the importance of the human not only in respect of human weaknesses but also in terms of the contingency of institutions. This importance is immense – there is almost nothing which does not have a historical origin and which therefore cannot return to it – and that is quite normal; the important thing is simply to avoid firing at every target of the acts of faith!

So it is unnecessary to take over in its entirety the witness which particular authorities at particular moments have made to themselves, their mission and their power. It is enough to respect them – and not to regard oneself as a prophet. Moreover, the word is so ineffective that one can almost always replace it by silence without inconvenience.

The only obligation that we enter into over faith is that of denouncing the lie, which produces universal corruption. Undoubtedly the lie takes on different aspects in the course of history: for sixteenth-century history, according to Erasmus, it was the discrepancy between appearance and reality; for nine-teenth-century Christianity, according to Kierkegaard, it was the difference between the social Christian and the Christian by faith.

In our time the lie can be seen more in disregard for humble but indispensable human realities, comprising all our toil and all our dignity, in the name of a 'supernatural' order. A clerical mentality, too often apologetic, authoritarian, protectionist and alien to culture, makes light of modest yet demanding intellectual attempts at verification, of the first steps in an ethical quest shared with our various brother and sister human beings, of the honourable and unchanging character of words public and private.

In order to sharpen our insight we should pay great attention to psychological and sociological approaches. They have much to

45

teach us and are frightening only because they shed so much light. They are most decisive when they are combined, because their 'interface' brings to light the social background to the church's presentation of a way of thinking, imagining and acting, illuminating the psychological background to its acceptance by the individual. Pure grace, the sheer verve of faith, cross these sticky morasses without losing their nature in them.

It is important to remember that the lie, 'bad faith', can be objective and institutional: it is then learned and put into practice, in all good faith, by people trapped by their own generosity. Sometimes, of course, one is tempted to think that the honesty of the moment has numerous intimate crimes as its foundation. But each of us has appealed often enough to the candour of our consciences, even when we have known that objectively we were wrong, so as not to have to admit the possibility that we have been misused and so as to avoid getting involved once again in a fight for the 'truth'.

The witness also makes his or her response from a tradition. To what degree? The important thing is to avoid half-measures as far as possible. One must welcome everything without eliminating anything, even 'heresies', in advance (there is to be no partial choice, no *hairesis*). The important thing is to reformulate, to recreate everything, depending on the distance from which it is separated from us by history. It is important to reinterpret and bring to bear the intellectual resources which are hidden in another culture. That is the price of faithful witness: anything that remains unchanged in a new context has been falsified, because it takes on a different meaning. The identical can only be rediscovered in otherness.

However, it is not enough to listen to everything and to try to give it new meaning. What we receive is so varied that it virtually falls apart. That is true even of the content of the 'orthodox' tradition and the New Testament, and if we try to bring it together it becomes contradictory and even absurd. We have to judge, to choose – Christians have always done this, though they have not been fully aware of the fact. In this second stage, heresy is not a question of taking a particular option but of altering the essential point: that God has entered human existence so that human beings can live as brothers and sisters with God.

For Catholics, the dogma was the adherence of the faithful to an integral and invariable system based on the absolute insight of the leadership, while the lure offered by others was the obvious message of scripture and its transparency to the individual Christian reader. There is no way of escaping relativity, change, choice, communal invention, the solitude of the believer.

Speaking only in his own name and not as the echo of some official doctrine, the witness must distinguish in his message between what is held in common within his church, what is held only by some, and what he himself believes. It is not a question of humility – tomorrow often proves a small number right – but of simple honesty. It is also an opportunity for freedom: I launch out more boldly if I know that the future of all witness is not bound up with the fate of my frail skiff.

Perhaps we expected the kingdom and landed up in the church? It would need a singularly narrow mind to see this as the answer to the questions raised by the annoucement of that kingdom. Perhaps the church, in its better aspects, might be seen as the lodging place of the small group around Jesus which tasted the signs of the kingdom and wrote down its harbingers in our history. But there is this cruel and vital difference: we know that everyday happenings are all that we can expect. My faith, my active welcome, my witness, are the only 'negative' that can reveal the kingdom here on earth.

4

The experience of the witness

Themes of witness

One does not plan to become a witness. Nothing is more puerile than the idea of adopting a certain kind of life in order to bear witness; nothing is emptier than the conversation of those who are obsessed with the need to proclaim their faith. It is simply a matter of existing – witnessing is given over and above that.

If witnessing is made up of long periods of fidelity to being and brief opportunities to speak about the secret of one's life when invited to, it makes a good deal of sense to take pains over this time of speaking, to direct this meditation on history, on the meaning of this faith which everyone is called to live out in his or her own way, towards a reflection on the act of communicating one's faith.

It is not easy to provide a complete justification for this concern and for my own interest in the question of witnessing. I feel it to be a kind of given, a responsibility which is directly bound up with the acceptance of faith and which is no more explicable than faith itself. I am made a potential witness - but this demand and preoccupation are not translated into proselytism or a desire to 'convert' others.

The simplest way of explaining it would be to refer to the experience of spiritual riches which, unlike other riches, cry out to be offered, to be shared. But that would not mean that it is a kind of intimate command which is in no way opposed to the discretion and patience involved in witnessing.

For one person, what he has discovered and would love to pass on to others, at the right moment, is the possibility of a humble happiness deep down which nothing can take away – though like everyone else he knows setbacks, suffering and solitude. This is a happiness which is not emotional contentment or personal distraction but the conviction and sometimes the feeling that the living heart of the world beats deep within him and within everyone else. For another person, it is the liberating certainty, the effective experience that in Jesus Christ, from God's side, a radical and unprecedented change in relations between human beings has become possible and that an earth inhabited by men of good will, the object of universal desire, is at least partially within our reach.

The gospel calls our attention to this. The authentic witness does not in any way flatter himself that his witnessing has borne fruit. There is a grace which permeates him, a demand which does not call for recognition in order to be satisfied. He does not complain of any ingratitude, does not feel hurt if the one whom he has aroused surpasses him in his gifts. He does not even rejoice at success but, rather, finds his cheerfulness in the experience and hope of his own faith.

The very thing to which he has been allowed to become a kind of public witness – one might say, rather hastily, a prophet, a saint – only keeps its authenticity if he continues above all to live and love, and if he speaks only in order to obey the law at the depths of his being. It is so easy to be caught up in being a 'seer', in the role, in the exaltation. But it is also easy to topple over! And in that way the religious novice could lose even the truth of his own existence.

The risk is all the more real when people of their own accord expect the witness to be exceptional – to kindle their imagination or to dispose them to imitate him. As if being faithful seriously, and in community, were not enough evidence of all the demands and marvels of faith.

So it is that Kierkegaard refused to call himself a Christian, because, in a society where everyone was thought to be one, this word could only be understood as a way of making oneself an exception, of claiming to be a saint. Confronted with an unbeliever he would not have hesitated to admit the fact, but no longer in a heroic sense. He would have stated it in an ordinary, modest way, doubting himself, if not the gospel, in the capacity of someone on the way towards... or trying to live as... Being a witness is precisely that.

His assurance

There are always militant believers who suggest that our word has become ineffective because it 'trembles': it is timid, hesitant, lacking the freedom of speech to which Paul is so fond of referring. I leave such incomparable assurance to those who sell ties, buy votes, preach in sects. As the reflection or echo of another word, which draws on the word of Another, my voice 'trembles', not from fear but out of respect for that to which I bear witness and by which I know myself to be completely eclipsed. In this kind of witnessing, audacity, reason would only prove only that one was off-target.

I am not even very concerned about my weaknesses: I would not defend them, but I no longer see them as a decisive hindrance. I know very powerful witnesses who are none the less imperfect: what counts is their faith, their effective goodness. I have to struggle against my weaknesses, but, if one thinks about it, an acknowledged lack of mastery over one's own image is quite a different kind of witness to the gospel from a discreet and tranquil satisfaction, or the groans and sighs prompted by a guilty conscience.

My assurance as a witness, like the certainty of my faith, is of the order of love. It is a matter of being confident that the other person will make the best choice, in his or her own way, sooner or later; it is a matter of respecting him or her for never having subordinated a unique destiny to the success of an idea or the aims of a group. It is a matter of being confident that my God loves and is capable of drawing everyone towards him, in particular along this remarkable way. It is a matter of trusting that the gospel of Jesus Christ can be a decisive, even inestimable, support for every man and every woman, even today, provided that they are allowed to take it up, in their own way, for this hour.

This assurance, unobtrusive though it may be, is deep and tranquil. Christian experience does not require us to feel disturbed and tense, living on our nerves. We remain quietly at home, at our ease: what we plant puts out roots, bears flower and fruit.

Such stability can help us to inhabit the earth, to put down human roots here. It is called for by the realization of the ultimate expectation, the incarnation. We are to live before God, with God, loving the countryside, a particular place, our home, the fields, the meadows and the orchards, our race, our family (either in the literal sense or as a metaphor for a culture) – welcoming, offering, sharing in the joy of a free heart.

But are not discontent, movement, the call of the desert, the status of the alien, the vocation of the pilgrim or the nomad – in short the Judaism of Abraham – more in accord with our anchorage in our God and his witness? We might ask other questions in reply. Are they a response to a revealed demand or to a kind of Judaism that is now half obsolete? Is this truly the only way of saving the otherness of biblical religion, of preventing it from lapsing into nature worship, folklore or myth, imprudent mysticism? Does not the alternative run risks in the opposite direction, of succumbing to the fascination of the most tainted, most puerile messianisms? So what has history to teach us? And what if the two have to exist side by side? Or if each of us has to experience them one after the other?

His particularity

Inevitably, my witnessing will be partial. Nor is the legitimate desire to be open to and to understand what is different – notably other religions – opposed to this particularity. On the contrary, it enables me to achieve it. I have my own voice, my own history, my own roots, even my own Christian experience. It is time to become aware of this; the dogmatic universality which rejects whatever is different without knowing anything about it and the philosophical universality which embraces it without retaining anything of its otherness are the opposed results of the same megalomania. As to syncretism, its approach and its limitations

51

must be seen as the result of spiritual mediocrity spirit and an illusory religious commitment.

The only universality is that which does not claim to embrace everything: the universality of expressions of humanity which are rich enough in meaning and beauty to be taken up and revisited indefinitely by others who can recognize much latent virtue in them and add yet more to bring them back to life. I have already spoken of a unique, ultimate, relevance of the Christian message.

In one way, if my witnessing is based on a sufficiently important experience, I cannot fail to be convinced that it has a universal value – in the sense that I have just mentioned: it is part of humanity. However, unlike a rational proposition, it cannot be given an entirely objective form; it cannot call for social recognition; it cannot become the basis of a power.

The idea that others can enrich and enlarge our knowledge of God without our ceasing to be ourselves is a very recent one, characteristic of the present-day encounter of religions. To live in blissful ignorance, to reject as worthless any contributions which are not derived from what one knows already, has always been the attitude of a variety of believers to one another, always with the exception of those who have been content to revere one god after another *ad infinitum*.

In any process of interchange the sharing of roots is essential. Unless we have an affinity to our conversation partners, share a common language, not to mention a common destiny with them, the drift of our witnessing tends to run out into the sand. We know that the yogi can 'awaken' the secular Western engineer, but the greater the difference, the greater the risk that the spiritual shock is in fact no more than an aesthetic one.

However, it is equally vital that the unity between two personalities should not be complete, that the difference between them should allow some detachment. Were this not the case, the gospel could be identified in a very dangerous way with each of the characteristics that conversation partners might have in common: simultaneous conversions to the Christian faith and to 'Action française' are familiar enough!

It seems that a community will only attract, and at all events can only integrate, men and women who have sufficient cultural and social conformity with it. Among the rare Christians who are very interested in the gospel, some have doubtless never been able to surmount the obstacles which make adherence to the faith so difficult today; others, who are perhaps more numerous, have not found a Christian group which can really receive them as they are.

At the same time, if the unanimity of a group goes beyond a certain point, it becomes closed and turns into a sect – despite any promises of outward sharing that it may make – and attracts only bigots and eccentrics. Without pursuing the mirage of a way in which every specific community can be universally effective, we can see that some experience of the unifying power of faith is indispensable to it. For others this discovery will be a sign of vitality which is far from being mediocre.

The witnessing community

We could discuss at length the reasons for the present demand for community. Be these what they may, the attraction exercised by living Christian communities, where they exist – lay or religious groups, local communities, reception centres with a few permanent members – is undeniable and quite understandable: they extend the witness of the gospel more than any individual could, or supplement the contribution of an exceptional personality.

As well as prayer – which could hardly become visible unless it were practised communally – people in fact discover here a quite amazing brotherhood, a welcome and a simplicity in communication. Sometimes, too, they find the rare combination of a deep commitment to the group and a real freedom from it. Moreover, many attractive features which, if noted in isolated individuals, could be derived from a particular personal truth, reveal their common inspiration if they appear more widely. Provided, that is, that they are not empty, forced, imitative, and that one does not learn six months later that the community has broken up, that its members have gone on to something else, that the whole enterprise has fallen into the void...

There are communities in which several members can also take the initiative in social or political action. Where this action starts from is significant for some time, even if it usually open to non-Christians and has no label nor any confessional control. For believers, there is an opportunity here to verify the impact of their faith on specific groups which Christian institutions can no longer provide everywhere. For others, this can be an occasion for questioning the absolute dogma – one hardly dares to say the prejudice – of religious alienation.

Can a married couple be such a witnessing community? To begin with, is this not what the couple are to each other? The faith of the one sometimes awakens that of the other at the time of marriage and the impetus can last and become mutual. However,it does seems to me that the type of reciprocal knowledge implied by the relationship of a married couple often diminishes their potential positive contribution, while as a general rule the disaffection of the one entails at least the practical disaffection of the other. That having been said, the married relationship is one of the ways of loving, of receiving, of acting together, which go beyond what either individual could represent or signify alone: to their children, to their kin, to those whom they meet. Though obviously a sign is not a cause...

The experience of having written, with two friends, several books expressing our experience as believers has given me some ideas about the relationship between 'I' and 'we' in faith which have a bearing on the communal character of witness. In works of this kind one has to welcome the different ways in which others express what one is ready to say; moreover, one discovers in oneself a kind of potential presence of aspects of the faith by which they live that are truly different. That this can happen also makes it possible to take other people seriously; here I leave on one side the problem of coping with specific differences which are irreconcilable. The more witnesses there are who are capable of recognizing each other, the greater the witnessing can become without being dissipated or neutralized.

However, as a general rule it is the similarity which proves to be most immediately significant. Thus radically opposed practices have all too often obliterated the message, and interpretations of it have been and have remained diverse to the point of cacophony.

Discordant practices must be firmly denounced, rather than being the subject of an episcopal negotiation which is in search of an impossible harmony; sometimes, without becoming proprietors of the eucharist, we have to refuse to share the bread. And it would be better to learn how to wait and understand than to brutalize, in the Roman style, undeveloped initiatives and suggestions: the damage done to witnessing in this way will remain real, even though no one may perhaps be responsible for it.

However, for those who escape fanaticism, the discovery of a kindred love of Christ in others who are very different and whose understanding of his person may even scandalize us can, in spite of everything, create a bond, a respect, an obscure brotherhood which bears witness in its own way, indicating a point of reference, a personal presence, which makes itself felt almost to the point of breaking meaning apart.

In a world where no one supports the Christian and where he carries all his baggage as yesterday's foundling, what is it that preserves him from the vertigo of unreality which seizes us when confronted with, say, astrology: a universe of representations the real content of which is nil? On the one hand, as I have said, there is the modest verification which consists in measuring the human creativity of faith by the wealth of our experience. And on the other hand there are exchanges within the community. Granted, these exchanges are not an absolute guarantee of anything, for collective aberrations are possible. However, they do allow us to cross a first threshold of plausibility, thanks to the conviction of one's travelling companions (despite the suspicion that everyone believes what the other believes) and their personal qualities (despite the fear of mass delirium).

Solitude and failure

In essentials, the believer is thrown back on the solitude of his faith which is also that of his witnessing. One can lighten the burden and share the joy, but to say 'I believe', whether in secret or in front of others, does not just arise out of an incommunicable decision: each time we find ourselves alone above 'thousands of feet of water', or in the middle of the desert, prey to the vertigo of a decision which is utterly foolish and nevertheless wise, tense yet peaceful, risky yet certain. To such a person, to acknowledge that seems to be even more burdensome than to offer it to his God; it is not longer my truth alone, my destiny alone in which I am involved – dare I reveal such a strange way?

At other times it seems quite simple. One says what one is, what one loves.

Solitude arises above all out of the ineffectiveness of our witnessing. That would be its failure if it had an aim; and it is in fact simply the reverse side of our helplessness. We are weak because the results we produce are never at our disposal; and even more, our solitude confirms our present inability to make what is dearest to us seem living, plausible or even comprehensible to our contemporaries.

We may have had occasion to assist brothers or sisters in the faith, to help to guide back to the faith friends who have long been alienated. Sometimes – and one confesses this less readily – we may have had to disturb the faithful, to watch the alienation of believers who were not very convinced. But how many times, when non-Christians have asked us questions, has our witnessing aroused in them more than interest or sympathy, or the good and obscure agnostic sentiment that something like that could well be true?

Thus the present nakedness of witnessing is not just because of the lack of any support from culture; it is a more difficult but less ambiguous condition – even an exhilarating condition, if faith can ultimately appear as the marvel among the 'more' that is offered to human desire, with its hunger beyond any conceivable need. This nakedness is also bitter frustration at being unable to communicate successfully, the barren sense of abandonment which overcomes us when the meaning that gives us life turns to nonsense as we utter it.

There is nothing intrinsically abnormal about the rejection of the gospel; the eventuality is foreseen, even inevitable – and we do not need to sound out people's hearts to know whether it is done by choice or blindly. So the proclamation of the gospel should have a vigorous effect in one of two directions, joyful acceptance or rejection, and provoke the 'crisis', the 'judgment', in which the judge finds himself judged. What is disturbing is the profound, almost universal, indifference that we encounter.

Could that be because we do not disturb ourselves in any way, because we do not interest or irritate anyone, because we are ineffective, and are thus dispensed from the supreme witness, the 'martyrdom', which seemed to Pascal, if not the sign of the truth of a cause – he was not so stupid as that – at least the indication that one believes enough to be ready to seal one's witness by the offering of one's life?

Our first brothers asked that they should be enabled to withstand the terrible temptation of the eschatological crisis, that of turning apostate when confronted with the threat of martyrdom. For us, only lesser temptations are left: to despair of God ever extricating us from all this misery, to be tired of always having to be on watch.

It is true that elsewhere people shoot Christians, flog them, exile them, torture them. It is irrelevant here whether that is because they belong to a politically-minded religious group. If an anti-Christian fanaticism is at work, the sense that individuals make of their sufferings or their death can be obscured for others by the consequences of a past in which their fellow-religionists have been unjust, conquerors or oppressors. If the gospel has led them to rebel against an intolerable social or political order, their martyrdom is complete, but it will be one with mixed motives, and there is a risk that only those who approve their struggle will recognize it.

Was it ever otherwise? Were not the Christians of the second and third centuries persecuted as members of a Jewish sect disturbed by messianic currents, and do some of their intransigences seem any more justified than the rejection of Chinese rites? By all means let us accept that in fact they were - we should nevertheless recognize that in all good faith a pagan could doubt this. Martyrdom can be an absolute necessity (and in that connection an authentic condition of witnessing), a decisive sign for other believers, something for everybody to respect – while remaining a very weak form of witnessing to outsiders. The harness does not hurt us when it is off our backs.

Let me say what I think, which may well be wrong: brotherhood attracts, charity turns things upside down, martyrdom strikes people; the absence or the lack of these things might seem an unsurmountable deterrent. But the touchstone is the question of God; it is that by which witnessing stands or falls. If God is not made present, or if this possibility does not interest one's conversation partner, nothing will emerge.

In one way, failure is sterile; Christian rhetoric which brings in the analogy of the cross on every issue begs the question. In another way the impotence of the witness – like religious anguish confronted with evil – can become an occasion for feeling to the full the strength of faith abandoning itself to the excesses of God: this matter is his affair. How could it depend on me whether or not the gospel is attractive and full of meaning, whether or not God bears witness to himself today in my witnessing and, with all the more reason, outside it?

The witness, condition for God

Certainly, without God, without the unpredictable God, nothing can happen. But this raises a question which is as obscure as it is decisive: is not our witness also an absolute condition for his manifestation? That would also imply that, deprived of our free co-operation, he could not bear witness to himself *in us*, and that *without us* he could not proclaim himself.

Without such a person, called by him, fallible, without such a group, indeed such a people, such a religion raised up by him and then falling back again, God still can. That is clear enough. He looks elsewhere, he finds: completely new believers, who emerge from nowhere; a new prophet; a new race of witnesses – provoking the 'jealousy' of the old and perhaps reviving it.

Is the appeal of this relay irresistible? Could these unexpected witnesses 'overlap' in such a way that if not their will and their intelligence, at least their free consent and loyalty were annulled? This produces a confused discussion in which Christian health, the distinctive accent of our faith, has always seemed to me to lean in a negative direction. However disproportionate our part might appear in this dual alliance, however artificial might seem the distinction between nature and grace, however great the unity

58

of gifts and vocation, in an individual or in a people – sometimes broken by the stupefying intervention of God in a corrupt or broken humanity – nothing could happen among us without our *fiat*.

What is still possible if no one gets up to say 'Here I am?' A sheer, blinding flash of divine power, a pure utterance of the 'Word' to a passive interpreter? Without a human spirit to welcome, to marvel at it, to interpret it, to want to hand it on, write it or pronounce it, what meaning would this miracle have for anyone? Nothing is said to man which does not go through man.

Moreover, in the history of religions, the claim to offer something radically new does not bear examination. Even when something new does seem to be on offer, the starting point is always an earlier witnessing. Noting this does not throw us back on the chimaera of a 'primitive revelation' or the illusion of the religious progress of humanity by successive new contributions and the selection of the best. It does force us to refuse to recognize breaks, really new developments. I would simply comment that to the need for an active witness we must add his or her dependence on those who have gone before.

If I were arguing, not as an irreplaceable being but as a *man*, not relying on anyone else and doing what I thought right as though there were no one but me, I would have to say: God could not bear witness to himself without me. But if this is my conclusion, can I succeed in getting beyond humiliation and guilt? Since I have come to understand that to acknowledge myself to be utterly surpassed by that which is the object of my witnessing is itself a condition of its manifestation, how can I avoid hiding away in terror? And if I saw my own presence as another of these conditions, and by no means the least decisive of them, would I not acquire a kind of pride, a grave feeling of being responsible for God? 'I say God when I say "I"' – and only I can do it.

I may be a Christian intellectual with a middle-class background, trained in existentialist thought and instinctively prone to defend the consistency of the individual subject; but I have learned enough and understood enough not to be too proud of that. I know that I have to check that the 'I' in question here, and indeed the very category of witnessing, does not imply a purely existential message addressed by one lucid subject to the clear conscience of another, whose passionate interest could be no more than an aspect of culture. In my view there is more to the 'I' than that, and the lack of mastery which I have had to accept affects not only the ineffable dimension of the witnessing, but also the psychological factors in me which welcome it, the image of it that I can accept and put forward.

It seems to me that the way in which many theoretical psychologists – outside schools centred on the ego – resort to the 'I' and to witnessing reinforces this way of looking at things. One could present all analysis as something that happens to the 'I': '*I* must arrive where *that* was'. Now since the verbal process which allows this to come into being is indirect and requires someone else to listen and interpret in order to bring to birth talk about desires which it has previously been impossible to express – often submerged within the symptom – everything depends on the testimony of the 'I'. The analyst neutralizes his social ego so that the 'I' in him can respond to the indirect discourse and become a witness, in the strict sense, to what is happening. In a weaker sense, one could say that the person being analysed is himself primarily a witness. But he reverts to this solely to recognize and accept what this does to him, to attest (in the fullest sense) to the analyst, in the first person, a certain 'truth' about himself which has only emerged at that point.

Moreover, above all in France, many psychoanalysts have been led by a mistrust of unconscious drives and the practical weakness of theoretical reconstructions to resort not so much to a pseudo-medical exposition of the case or a systematic elaboration of it, as to the primacy of experience (what the unconscious throws up in analysis and self-analysis) and to noting testimony addressed to a hearer or a reader in whom a resonance has been felt.

The presence of the witness

The personal presence of the one who bears witness also raises problems of another order. Encounter with a living witness, whose life backs up his testimony and who 'stands by his word', is so essential that people have been able to deny any other form of witness. There is in fact a good deal of illusion in the narration or the diffusion in book form of the lives and miracles of past witnesses, in a culture in which the unconditional faith of the narrator and the prestige of a writing from a distant past no longer bear any resemblance to what they were.

A contemporary might perhaps add that every transmitted text derives from a variety of unverifiable meanings which disguise the event or the original experience. But is that not a dogmatic, pseudo-scientific decision about language? Does only the living word escape the blind functioning of language? Cannot interpretation, creative though it may be, revive for others human thought and experience which has been put down in writing? Do we read a page of Plato, Paul or Montaigne as we would look at an Aztec or Egyptian bust?

If we adopted a more sophisticated position, we might accept that an author speaking of himself and what he has 'seen and heard' can make himself present, and bear witness – I mentioned this hypothesis at the beginning of this book. I said there that what is needed is talent, since the literary medium imposes its own inexorable laws. We should also add the achievement of a union between the writer and the believer, which is rarer still. The same conditions, and genius on top of that, are required to bring others to life (in the strict sense): the account must make the witnesses of whom it is speaking *live*. But in the end it is the conviction of the narrator which plays the decisive role and perhaps constitutes a real personal witness: he *signs* it.

Sometimes the writer has sought only to be a narrator and has found himself credited with a commitment which he did not intend or did not dare to make. But this equivocation is compensated for by the innumerable cases in which one reads as a mere fable something that was written with flesh and blood.

There is no way in which witness can be anonymous. The exegete who affirms that originally, in the New Testament, all witness was anonymous, proves nothing, and he cannot conceal the theory that makes him argue this: it is that testimony does not derive from an empirical and incontestable fact, but from a *faith* which opens up for us a possibility of believing. Such a person is not entirely wrong – but he forgets that this possibility is not just suggested by spoken words but is manifested in an experience where it has become reality. It is necessary for someone who introduces himself and gives us his name, to show us that for him a way has effectively been opened.

Nor is that all. Certainly we begin from a fact, not empirical but historical. This fact is that of a first basic experience, an experience which the later believers could not have again in the same way, one which was handed down to them by a known chain of witnesses. It was the experience of those who had been together 'all the time that the Lord Jesus went in and out among us, beginning from the baptism of John until the day when he was taken up from us'. They had not had *direct* access to that to which they bore witness, any more than their successors, though their successors may have believed that they did, but it was given them to see the Witness 'with their eyes, and touch him with their hands'.

We have no assured knowledge of his experience and his inner life, but we know by the words that have come down to us or by the trace that he has left in those who have followed him and who have described him to us – sometimes attributing their own stories and thoughts to him – the life that he offers us from the life which he himself lived. The drift of this indirect yet decisive witness of Jesus is confirmed if we believe that God, towards whom he directs us, can also be sensed in his human existence, regardless of what awareness Jesus himself may have had of this unique manifestation.

Certainly he was a witness who was effectively present, known by his name, speaking in the first person, at a particular time, in a particular place, within the constraints of his humanity. One cannot use the trans-historical significance of his message, the mystery of his person, to transform him into a superman, the gnostic saviour figure which has existed in every age, knowing everything, having lived out in embryo each of our experiences. But it would also be wrong to reduce him to his social role at that time or to the understanding that his first disciples had of him. Creativity remains: there is much to learn and to say. A curious fact is that these potential riches often tend to reveal themselves to interpretation, in actions and in words, when one is called to bear witness to him in unprecedented situations rather than in simple meditation.

The genesis of faith in witnessing

And so it is that in spelling out the approach to witnessing as an added factor, which was my starting point, I have had to bring out another of its facets. It can happen that in trying to express our faith to someone else, we discover in ourselves an understanding that we did not think we had; we find a power of expression so unexpected that in this way more than one person overcomes the doubts he or she thought they had.

The profound inner resonance that this arouses in us dissuades us from seeing this new power, this affirmation, as so many effects of a desire to convince or to affirm. It is perhaps this advent of faith in the process of bearing witness that the first Christians saw as the presence of the Spirit in the men and women who were called to 'give account of the faith which is in them' – in this case not as a miracle, but as a law of this paradoxical communication.

On the one hand it is the law of a personal progress. The need for me to prepare to bear witness or actually to testify clarifies and refines my perception. The very fact that the other person is different requires me to go further. He does not share with me the unverified evidence that a perceptive brother in the faith can offer me, so I am forced to take account of the cultural gap which divides us from the ancient expressions of this faith, that can only be surmounted by the invention of a new language. Now when I embark on this process of creating afresh, what I am doing is to bring out the hidden riches which the message still contains. That is, provided that I accept the risks of this dialogue; that I do not take refuge in repetition; that I allow myself to be affected by the surprise of the other person; that I do not declare myself satisfied before arriving at the best expression possible.

It is a matter of listening to the other person. Our present condition offers us a decisive opportunity. We must meet head on the demands for historical credibility, for the revision of precritical metaphysics, for verification by praxis, for confrontation with other religions, that all our contemporaries share – albeit after the fashion of Monsieur Jourdain. That is, provided that these demands are not bound up with a communication block for which the blame cannot be laid at our door: unsurmountable prejudices, hostility disguised as a rigorism held to so firmly that there is no room for any other human conviction or decision, or absolute indifference. In that case analysis and reformulation will only end up in a further impasse and in the failure that I have already mentioned.

This, then, is what I find as I speak and write. First, there is the feeling of being incapable of expressing in a meaningful way something that nevertheless fires me; or more often, the impression of finding myself empty and without anything to say. That gradually gives way to the birth of words, written words, which bear witness and actually evangelize me. They do so not only in the customary sense of teaching me to be consistent with the word that I convey, on pain of losing it, but also, more radically, in making me discover my own faith.

On the other hand, this is the law of a singular Revelation. Perhaps I could say that something of what one wants to bear witness to emerges only in the act of witnessing. That the word of God is only grasped in its meaning for today, only makes sense, only shows its modern face (the sole access to an eternal truth which transcends the variety of cultures has not been written down in a timeless formula but allows itself to be felt in a series of approximations) by expressing itself and acting as a word of salvation, of pity, of hope for specific human beings, at a given time? Then and only then, perhaps, a veil lifts, a mystery becomes transparent which is simply that of love. That would ultimately make witnessing the supreme place of Manifestation.

5

Relations between believers and non-Christians

Believers: removing some misunderstandings

The subject of modern unbelief, its history, its reasons and its types, has been virtually exhausted. I propose here only to describe and try to understand the relationship between Christians and non-Christians, their attitudes, what they think of one another, in so far as they constitute the specific setting for our condition as witnesses. To begin with, I shall attempt to diagnose the misunderstandings which constantly arise. It seems to me that believers are almost entirely responsible for them. People would not want us to give our own doorstep only a quick once-over.

In our century believers are no different from non-believers in their external life-style; they live together and communicate with one another in all situations of private or public life. However, believers have failed to carry on a satisfying conversation about the nature of their own basic convictions and those of their non-believing neighbours; in particular they have failed to talk about the acceptance or the rejection of Christian faith. I think that Christians often speak ill of non-believers and of themselves: non-believers find it very difficult to recognize themselves in what is said about them and sometimes to understand or accept what believers want to make them admit about themselves.

The first basic error is always to begin from Christianity and to judge others in terms of it, as a result calling them unbelievers. I would say that that is a mistake, not if it is a matter of evaluating a difference or of understanding oneself, but if one is trying to have some idea of the way in which other people understand themselves. More often than not, they will not even think of calling themselves unbelievers, and if they do so, they will not be saying anything about themselves which they feel to be essential. Moreover, because the term 'unbeliever' is so sweeping, they will not think it an appropriate indication of the very different degrees of not adhering to Christianity and the reasons behind them; and because it is negative, it will not seem an appropriate way of describing the convictions they really want to talk about and the mark these convictions have left on them.

The second mistake arises from an inability to tolerate the questions posed to Christian conviction by a determined and honest unbelief; the tendency is sometimes to reject and sometimes to take over the other person in order to remove the difference. Faith exerts so much pressure that unbelief is made to seem guilty where it is not.

Hence some notorious bigots, one who died a cardinal – he used to be fond of repeating that atheists physically repelled him – and two or three others who are still alive, have written that atheism has always been the fruit of sin. In their view, the 'good conscience' which accompanies it in fact bears witness only to a conscience which has been more or less willingly distorted. Atheism, they say, is born of pride and rebellion, or of the bad faith which is often a cloak for bad morals; it is the inevitable source of despair and of the destruction of a human being. Some non-Christians, having unfortunately become aware of this literature, have found no difficulty in denouncing the prejudice, the error, the injustice in it.

A first variation on this approach is to accept the perfect sincerity of those many non-believers who never discovered the gospel or for whom Christianity was only a childhood religion, soon contradicted by their experience as men and women. However, people taking this line will deny that it is possible to 'lose faith' in all loyalty if one has been a convinced Christian. Since God is faithful, there must have been some secret failing which blotted out this light of which one had once counted the cost; alternatively, here might be a sign that someone had only seemed to believe.

Without going so far as to sound out consciences, it is evident that such arguments are the development of an *a priori* position, and the witnessing of many people whose honesty we have no reason to suspect makes it seem crazy.

Then there is a second variation. This approach holds that the various forms of atheism – scientific, political, humanist (people like these florid analyses) – are based on a conviction which, while sincere, often disguises its anti-religious passion by giving it the form of a theoretical argument or presenting it as what proves to be the opposite of the wager of faith. Now if it is true that the unbeliever, to use a phrase of Marie Héraud's, is the one who says a clear no to Christianity as he knows it, then his choice is made without any hostile passion. In fact, in the vast majority of instances in our day, there is no social pressure on him or her to adhere to the Christian faith, and in the intellectual sphere there is no need to come to a decision on the question as though it were a vital crossroads.

On the other side we have the generous comments of those for whom the non-believer is always more or less a believer without knowing it, since, they say, in pursuing his quest for the absolute he desires God without knowing it, and it is by good faith that he remains in error. Simply by his right conduct he has indeed found God without succeeding in naming him; he often recalls to believers Christian truths which have 'gone to seed' because he has rediscovered them and practised them when they were lost or neglected. But does not elementary respect for others require us to accept them as what they claim to be? Is every quest a quest for the absolute? And is every absolute religious? How do we know whose behaviour is 'right'? And what human rectitude is capable of leading us to God? Have not people been far too ready to stress the Christian origin of attitudes which many of our contemporaries have learned outside that current, and sometimes against it? When we turn to the subject of guilt, for example, of dolorism, or of a defence of feebleness and resignation, a defence is manifestly slower to emerge.

And there is a variant from which I accept that *The Time of Patience* was not entirely immune. When we note the impasse in which witnessing finds itself and analyse the reasons for it, we

67

always presuppose to some degree that others do not know the true Christian faith. What we ought to admit, though we do not really want to do so, is our belief that if they did see the true faith they could not fail to accept it or at least to love it. Now on the one hand, this position appeals to a possible Christianity with which we identify – an ideal form of Christianity, because it conforms with our aspirations and, we think, with those of our conversation partners. Whereas what they see is a real Christianity, down through history and in the present. When that bears down on them with all its weight, how far should they credit our protests, our dreams? On the other hand, how do we know that they do not understand our faith all too well and keep away from it knowing quite clearly why they do - though that does not make them rebels or sorry figures? Perhaps indeed they constantly devote themselves to the same basic human values which are our concern.

We must accept our disquiet when confronted with such observations, if we find them convincing, just as we expect our conversation-partners to live with the problem posed to them by the discovery to which Valéry gave classic expression and which they found at least as unexpected as ours. They sometimes have to tell themselves that there are believers who are neither stupid nor mad, nor more deceitful nor less human than they are. No encounter is possible without this reciprocal amazement.

A better-known variant, of a very different kind, always plays down the reasons that others have for not believing, blunting the point, disguising the consensus. I would suppose people to do this to reassure themselves and to get closer to others, rather than in order to launch an attack on their unbelief. Here are some examples. Scientific atheism is on the decline, it is said, along with impeccable explanations of the universe – yes, but the scientific method hardly matches the approach taken by faith, and the results of science make religious representations obsolete; God will never return to being the missing key. The different forms of atheism are in conflict and neutralize one another, it is said – except for agreeing on one obvious thing: atheism. Faith can adapt to the Copernican revolution produced by the Kantian critique of knowledge, it is said, if this latter can remedy its inherent weakness, namely, that of barring our access to 'being' – but that is what made it Copernican! Exegetes no longer deny the historical existence of Jesus, it is said – now we all simply argue that it is impossible to reconstruct his life or to attribute any particular saying to him with certainty. How can one avoid a situation where 'the sincerity or the intelligence of the believer always seem doubtful to the non-believer'?

In a more subtle way, instead of anathematizing or taking over the position of others, one can either stress the difference or try to remove it – again in an attempt to bridge the gap. In the first case the approach will be to stress the absolutely free gift of faith or the purely voluntary nature of decision – here the wager, indeed the absurd, is the criterion. It will be to stress an utterly transcendent Revelation which carries with it a complete vision of humanity, the opposition between faith and religion sheltering the former from the humane sciences to which the latter are abandoned. What does it matter that this ship, riding high, is letting in water everywhere? People bail it out with dignity – or sink...

At the opposite extreme are the many Christians who affirm that there is a believer *and* an unbeliever within them, that the frontier runs through each one of us. That is subjectively true of those who do not know whether they are one or the other, or who move alternately from one condition to the other. However, for many others the formula is rhetorical: it simply expresses the intrinsic dimension of uncertainty or doubt which exists *within* faith, but does so in such a way that they feel their isolation, their strangeness, to be attenuated. Now in both cases non-believers reject such language outright. On the one hand, they feel no division of this kind within themselves. And on the other, they are very well able to recognize Christians, no matter what such people may claim – if only by their explicit or implicit reference to the person, the message or the text to be found at their origin. So often (though not always) other people see us more clearly than we see ourselves; not as a result of the image that we present, but by our undeniable actions and words.

We are not to think ourselves more nor less than others. We must be aware that the believer and the non-believer are both human beings: the only difference is faith or its absence. We must understand that if our culture is the same, our characteristics with regard to religion will also be the same: a sort of zero starting point (while this lack of religion may not be 'natural', it is at least cultural, a successor to the common religious feeling of the past). This leads to comparable difficulties, regardless of whether they are felt in the faith or outside it. We are to seek to live out the same positive human experiences, embark on the same intellectual adventures as the 'modern world' (that is not an empty word, nor is it a eulogy), cherish the same hopes and involve ourselves in the same just struggles. We have heard all this a hundred times. But how many people in the church have risked it?

That having been said, understood and put into practice, the essential difficulty remains. How do we get out of the specific cultural isolation that is brought about by one-way communication? We may take up the ways in which our friends look at things and their reasons for living, and share them to some degree, but in doing so we shall not manage to give them any indication which satisfies us as to why we still hold to the faith. We may even have found that the more we try to make them understand, the greater their perplexity becomes.

The hope of a productive exchange depends on this one presupposition: that within *each* of us, as Christians, an inner dialogue is going on between the sense of belonging, the atmosphere, the tradition of faith and the understanding, practice, even the passion of *that particular* area of the present quest in which living people are involved (new forms of education, for example, and also yoga); that there is in *all* of us an overall sensitivity to the most important of those approaches which make up the fabric of our culture. And such approaches can have a relationship to the Christian heritage which is both critical and positive.

If we are to see things clearly, we need to move from a consideration of bodies of texts and conversation between firmly established positions (like that of the psychoanalyst with his 'compulsory' atheism and that of the Christian with his 'specific' anthropology) to a loyal confrontation that individuals initiate themselves, *qua* individuals. Then we need to move from a renewed interpretation of the faith made by someone who from that point on is assimilated to the secular world and often invisible to it, to an encounter with a non-believing analyst quite different from the one I mentioned earlier, the value of which would be that he could recognize the work latent in it and one day might perhaps say, 'If I believed, it would be like that.' There are four stages, the story of a life. Is that too complicated? But how many of those things in life that really matter are easy?

Père Chenu once told me that the first condition is to renounce all indoctrination. If non-believers ask me a question about Christian teaching, I should not reply directly, but use what I know about them to see how I can help them to advance along their way. As I listened to him, I thought what a great sacrifice it would be for many people to deprive themselves of the pleasure of explaining, and also how careful one must be not to fall into the trap of discussing the present state of religion - discussions which satisfy curiosity and stifle all possible interest. Finally, another form of respect is to say honestly what one thinks without bothering to know why the other is asking and what it will mean for him or her. One of these two approaches will prove best – depending on circumstances.

Père Chenu went on to say that the second condition would be to recognize the values of the non-believer – or those most basic to his quest. I asked him, 'Would you also say that of his unbelief?' 'As far as I am concerned,' he replied, 'he has a belief. If he is agnostic, he teaches me just how many difficulties there are and how deep the Mystery is, far more effectively than many believers. From then on this Mystery brings us together, even if he can make nothing of it – and his position is a warning that I should not try to manipulate God. For faith is just as much questioning,' he concluded, 'as consent.'

There are specific obstacles to such dialogue, but to a large extent its difficulty is that of all communication: getting beyond an exchange of information, an attempt to be appreciated, the pleasure of referring to the same culture, the fear of betraying our weak points; arriving at a certain mutual expression of what we feel to be essential to us. It is quite a different effort from the one we have to make to express our most personal feelings. Sometimes it calls for the long patience of a friendship with some rather grey evenings which nevertheless knows its times of grace; sometimes true words will be spoken at a chance encounter.

Now and then, such a sharing of vital questions leads to soemwhat unexpected discoveries, which must be taken into account, even if no definitive character is attached to them. For believers, this will be some obliteration of the awareness of a difference, which I have already mentioned in another context. This undoubtedly develops from the backlash of an increase in 'Christian specializations' and the realization that Christians and non-Christians share many essential questions and most of the replies that can be given to them. Among non-Christians, religious questions are to some degree submerged, though not entirely abolished (this point is rightly stressed by Jacques Sommet), and people are reticent about becoming personally involved in them; this is a reticence to which we shall have to return later in this chapter. We have all had this experience: the purpose of a meeting is a confrontation between faith and unbelief and soon the conversation turns to something else which is of great interest to both sides – and all the starting points are completely confused.

I spoke earlier of sharing the same expectations and the same struggles. A true exchange might often begin today with an honest pooling of disillusionment, with the courageous recognition of failure: the failure of science, of progress, of liberalism, of socialism, of Christianity to make the human life of most of our fellow men and women less precarious and less insignficant. It might begin with a lucid criticism – saddened, I hope, but not sarcastic – of total explanations, of rational or dogmatic thoughts which never miscarry.

Perhaps it might also begin with the decision to make a new start together on these intellectual efforts and these struggles for uncertain results, but from now on without dreams. Though one might suppose that Christians were bad travelling companions because of their rigidity, and the finer points of their morality

72

would make them be scrupuluous about their actions, however necessary these might be, they might well prove to be trained to be more tenacious than others in hopeless causes which nevertheless make a great deal of sense.

There is one point that I have already touched on which must be taken up again in this context. That is a kind of agreement on the need we find to resort to others, to bring out differences, a reflected taste for relationship. This is what we require for every human advance, and for more than that. It may well be that others give me adequate light – God is big enough for that; they may also simply prompt me to resume my own course: without them my ultimate quest might lose momentum. There are enough reasons here for breaking with the illusion of purely internal paths, the reassurance of only meeting one's kin, the lack of active interest in discovering others, the laziness which hinders the arrangement of fruitful meetings.

There is one last condition, which has two aspects. It is hardly worth mentioning, but the majority of priests or religious have done little to verify it, nor are they the only ones. This condition is first and foremost a complete indifference to social hierarchies: the important thing is that people should understand that for you a human being is a human being, neither more nor less. What stands in the way of this is your penchant for accepting flattery and the pride you take in it (this is a bourgeois remnant of the sacralization of earlier days); or, more rarely and more subtly, the inverted snobbery that prompts your friendship with common people; or, finally, your soberly scornful manner towards people without interesting minds.

That amounts to a total elimination of Pharisaism: of social judgment disguised as moral judgment, and even of the application of this latter to others on the basis of personal principles. It is important to accept the other as he is (as they say, to accept is not to approve), and that is a first important stage. However, it is necessary to go further: not to judge anything and only to decide – whether you speak or keep silent – what you would like to do yourself. There is no contradiction between the absence of any condemnation of others and the utter assurance of one's own ethical convictions. On this point it is possible to have a dialogue

73

with most of our contemporaries, to transcend the most odious aspects of the received images of Christianity, and finally to arrive at the very vision of God to whom we can bear witness.

Non-believers: some attitudes to faith or to Christians

Today the relationship between Christians and non-believers is one of uncertainty; near as one may be to people, one does not always know what they think about God or about Christianity, and often they do not know themselves. What is left once one is 'no longer a Christian'? Sometimes I try to convince myself, in conscious reflection or as the echo of one of my words, that many people still have a secret interest, an expectancy. And sometimes I feel that this interpretation is no more than wishful thinking: it seems to me to plumb the depths of indifference and alienation.

Be this as it may, experience has taught me, sometimes brutally, that a large number of friends who would not call themselves Christians do not want to be described in negative terms, swept up into the group of 'unbelievers'. They cannot fix their position in that way. The formula that I have used, that we must accept people on their understanding of themselves, may prove useful for doing away with all attempts at recruitment by redefinition, but it certainly does not get to the bottom of things. People carry around questions, not to mention attachments, which are no longer comprehensible and which perhaps only specific circumstances can bring out. It is even conceivable that they do not want to, or are unable to, speak about things of which they are aware, since the word is not a simple act and can cloak a great many functions. Even blasphemy is a remarkably complex matter.

Certainly hatred of God exists, but more as ambivalence or a 'temptation' to exclude him than in the form of the anti-theism which was so virulent in the last two centuries. The pressure to believe is no longer so strong that doubt in the goodness of God or in his respect for human dignity and freedom is followed by atheism. Atheism is sometimes militant, even among the young, but this is in a concern to efface the 'noxious' traces of the church or of Christian ideas; it lacks the passion which formerly ranged

74

ex-believers against a figure who was detested more than he was denied.

Attitudes towards religion present a motley picture: Christians detached from a community; non-practising believers; Christians who have great difficulty with the faith or the church, many of whom call themselves 'disbelievers'; practising Christians completely ignorant of the gospel; anti-clerical figures of the old kind; adherents of other religions or attracted by them; convinced atheists; agnostics. However, the dominant feature is beyond question indifference: alienation, the strangeness, the absence of all thought on the subject and the utter ignorance of the majority of young people.

If we listen to the most thoughtful of non-believers, they give two reasons for the alienation induced in them by religions and particularly our own (they do not explain their lack of faith: reasons are no longer needed today for a failure to adhere to the gospel, and other, quite different, ones are needed to abandon it). In my view these reasons are the same as those which were already produced, in a different way, in the middle of the eighteenth century. First, people argue, religions are primarily based on intolerance, and they point to the hatred engendered by religions in history, the source of separation between those who continue with them. Secondly, they point to the way in which Christianity has been hostile to life, to earthly joy, to the body, to sexuality, to women – an attitude which, with very minor qualifications, is still characteristic of those in authority.

These charges are justified if one thinks of the great claims made by the church, that it is the creator of peace, the embodiment of humanity. All the same, one might suppose the criticism to be superficial: Christian faith did not create either hatred or gnosticism. At the very most the churches have been guilty of engaging in power games and endorsing the divisions of the world instead of fighting them, of justifying guilt and the fear of living instead of assuaging them. It might be more appropriate to be amazed at the fact that again and again the gospel has raised up prophetic protest and happy thanksgiving on this earth.

Doubtless it would be more thoughtful to note, with others, that even when Christians understand the importance of effort and struggle here on earth, they only commit themselves with the tips of their fingers: in their eyes such commitment is less than essential or definitive, and remains within the realm of means and ends: it is the underside inevitably associated with any trasncendent vision. Such a view might be more profound, but it is less true: things might have been like that, but they are no longer so – leaving aside, perhaps, some neo-conservative groups which I have already mentioned. We are in fact under pressure from the opposite temptation, to love the earth for God's sake to the point of forgetting him.

Finally, very often the non-believer supposes the Christian to be fearful and repressed. The Christian is supposed to be someone who tries to put his mind at rest, who has been able to escape the most difficult problems, who wants to escape ungrateful reality and solitude, who hands things over to others. He is someone who is constrained by a web of dogmas which he never questions and who finds that every way forward, every possible opening, is blocked.

Might not this description be truer if people refrained from generalizations? But in that case questions might arise which they would prefer to avoid. That is why in this kind of confrontation – as in that between religions or Christian confessions – so many people look for what is most contrary to them, what conforms integrally with the way in which it is defined – however absurdly – and does not shift. This, they say, is what they respect (though in fact it may give them a salutary shock) – this is sound and courageous. This is what provides the two partners with their social landmarks and excuses each of them from asking questions.

What question would a non-believer be led to ask if he accepted that quite a large number of Christians escape such a criticism? Might he have to become a believer himself? That is rather too simple. He would have to confess a degree of disquiet, to ask questions about Christianity. But this disquiet is more disturbing to the believer who discovers it: here, to his amazement, he is confronted by a man or woman, whom he now knows and of whom he thinks highly, and who yet must be supposed to believe – in nothingness! And if we investigate the basic testimonies to this faith – as I have noted – the incomprehension grows. Can someone base his or her life in this way on what irrefutably proves to be a collection of very ancient myths and legends?

It is not just the classical discussion of evil which bears witness to this alienation between the conversation partners. A great many non-believers hardly refer to this major difficulty, and cite it less and less as a reason for their rejection of Christianity. However, what was once the sphere of conflict was also that of dialogue, and as we know, while Christianity has no 'acceptable' solution, it is not without resources for dealing with the question. We cannot say that the problems are continuing to disappear, for there are also believers who affirm that this set of questions has become strange to them. We should simply note that the points of contact are rarer.

Though it may be true that 'hard' believers and unbelievers provide mutual support for one another, there is a second area of understanding which is hardly less paradoxical. There are historians, sociologists and philosophers who detect with delight the presence of religion in a large number of 'secular' patterns of behaviour in our time – without believing themselves. They have no difficulty in agreeing on this point with Christian apologists, at the cost of a serious distortion of ideas and sometimes of facts. I am thinking here of the analysis of cultural factors as 'transposed religion'. To recognize certain mythical or ritual elements in political or sporting scenarios – to broaden the concept of religion to embrace all faith, all salvation, all visions of the absolute, even if they are purely this-worldly or ideal – is a rather more dangerous undertaking for the understanding of religion and indeed for the understanding of all other human activities.

On the other hand, what needs to be understood – for this observation allows us to separate quite different areas of sensibility in the matter of witnessing – is that once our tendency towards sheer unbelief is abolished, the conviction of personal religion – whether cultivated or popular – is not universal. This trait may be found in France, in the Iberian peninsula, and to a certain degree in Italy, Germany and Scandinavia, but it is absent from the Anglo-Saxon world, where a vague religious element remains a feature of industrial and social life.

Whereas some non-believers may still pass a generally severe verdict on the Christian religious tradition, others, having distanced themselves and expressed their reservations on certain past presentations or patterns of conduct, are more positive. They see the richness of Christianity, the way in which it is an essential root of our culture. Granted, the aspects which are endorsed in this way can differ widely: Christianity may be seen as a necessary stage, an admirable inspiration for art, the foundation of morality, an irreducible affirmation of the person, a source of social order or recurrent dissidence, fine myths which are still creative, a pure movement of faith which remains indispensable once it has been purified of all content, the exemplary figure of Jesus, and so on. As at the end of the eighteenth century – after the polemic of the Enlightenment – there is a tendency to regret its decline, to measure the void that its absence creates.

To be known, to be esteemed – even while being regarded as in some respects obsolete – seems preferable to putting up with blind opposition. We might also ask whether this is a stumbling block, or a definitive vaccination against all new discoveries. However, is a *complete* ignorance of Christianity, of the kind that we find among some Western Europeans under thirty, a position so far beyond this post-Christian situation that eventually there is a sense of a completely fresh curiosity, a promising development, or does our cultural zero rule out the last possible ways that might be taken?

What I am in fact asking is whether a religion can ordinarily come to individuals other than through a tradition which, if not that of a family, is at least that of a culture. But what about the evangelization of Africa? Was not the superior intellectual development of Christianity, and of Europe, the decisive factor? And what about Asia? Is not the failure of Christianity proof of this, leaving aside some ambiguous situations or some individuals capable of uprooting themselves, of discovering the difference? But what about late antiquity, through which the faith was spread? Was not the cultural homogeneity between the presentations of Christianity and the surrounding world greater than that of today, and to ensure that this should be greater, did not people pay the price of a Hellenization or a Romanizing of the Christian faith, a price so great as to be beyond the means of a religion as differentiated as it is at present? I am certainly not drawing conclusions: my hope is for quite the opposite: the verve and the resources of a new hey-day. But I have to ask these questions, to point up the difficulties.

Among the non-believers who are closest to us – though separated from us by all the distance between atheism and faith – there are those who in their creation are in search of an absolute, which they dream of as an ideal perfection outside this world. They may claim that this is impossible, or they may want to incarnate it in the here and now, in finitude, while knowing it to be paradoxically ephemeral. The Absolute is what it is by the indefinite openness that it evokes, by the way in which the questioning, the waiting, is over and above any conceivable answer, any conceivable result. One might call such people 'religious', indeed they might adopt that term themselves were the equivocation not dangerous, but the affinity is there all the same. Others, in an unlikely way, would call 'God' the blank sheet, the void before them which makes them go forward in their actions, the boundless, infinite emptiness of the future.

While it may be non-Christians who in fact think that nothing makes sense and that nothing is left but enjoyment, or even that no meaning is to be found in the world and that we must try to make meaning in it ourselves, though perhaps recognizing the immanent tendency in all life, others will constantly want to evoke a 'presence' of being, of value, of meaning, of unity, received and given, whether or not it is affected by an absolute coefficient. Many people try to elucidate the significance of the word God as a possible key to this uncertain quest. Some even find themselves in the grips of this word and expect it to prove its power.

One strange fact, which has been verified many times, is that one can love God without believing in him – and sadly, one can believe in him without loving him.

So it comes about that people have an ardent desire to pray without actually doing it, for want of believing; that people pray without knowing whom they are addressing; that they learn to meditate without finding it more than a beneficial silence; that atheists have a mystical experience, with many of its traditional connotations.

79

Some people have said or written that while they themselves are not sufficiently certain to commit themselves to faith, in a way they believe in those who believe. Are these people to be credited with a sincerity, an authenticity, a quality of being which *must* signify something else? Are we to hope, even if we do not dare to claim, that their faith really reaches that on which it is orientated?

There may be agnostics who are basically sceptical, but there are in fact a large number of others who keep on asking whether there might not be something vital about this matter of faith. But they do not succeed in discovering sufficiently decisive reasons for taking one step further, all the more so when confronted with all the dubious aspects of the history of Christianity. I know people who have gone so far as to give their children a religious education so that they shall really be in a position to make a choice, knowing that in our present context, 'leaving them free to make up their minds later', and abstaining from doing anything to prepare them, means that in all probability nothing will ever happen.

The whole lives of some of these men and women revolve around the faith, the church, with the best will in the world – one would think – and yet they do not end up there. Why? And why have we been able to believe?

Witness and witnessing in
the church

Who is a witness for his companions on the way?

In my meditation on the relationships involved in witnessing I
have above all had in mind the encounter of Christians and non-
Christians, and I then went on to indicate its specific features. At
the same time, however, I have said what I could about the way
in which believers can bear witness to one another. All that I need
do here is to bring together, as briefly as possible, some features
which relate to this latter situation.

For centuries, the 'saints' of former days have been the
witnesses *par excellence* for Catholicism – through their 'heroic
virtues', the miracles which they performed or obtained, or their
'canonization effected by the church'. They have been signs of
the passing of God, points of reference to structure Christian life
and give rhythm to the liturgical year; they have been intercessors,
friends. It is probable that the sudden obliteration of the saints is
connected partly with a historical awareness of the legends,
artifices and omissions which have contributed to the development of these typical figures, and partly with the complex political
stakes involved in their official recognition. But beyond question
we must also connect this development even more with a return
to the basic figures and events of the faith, and above all with the
feeling that we are too remote from them, as much by the
difference in time as by the dehumanization which hagiography
inevitably brings with it.

We have never been more aware of the need of present-day

witnesses. We want to hear about them against the background of the world in which they too confronted existence and lived out their faith; we want to make these witnesses of old to whom we return in some way our own, by rediscovering their features and showing that they were more vulnerable, more fraternal. Above all we want to show that they are approachable, offering that surplus value of direct experience over and above the story to which I have already alluded.

Who are the public figures alive today – or those who have lived in modern times and who are still remembered – to whom Christians refer? For want of a serious study, I shall simply mention several names that come to mind: very different, always more complex than their legends tend to indicate, sometimes really ambiguous and – most important of all – active in a limited number of areas. There are witnesses of courage and hope: Martin Luther King, Oscar Romero, Guy Riobé. There are witnesses of goodness and active compassion: John XXIII, the Abbé Pierre, Mother Teresa. There are witnesses of miracles made possible: Padre Pio, Marthe Robin. There is the witness of the right attitude and the right word in a situation of unbelief and distress: Dietrich Bonhoeffer. There is the witness of an assurance which strengthens Christians humiliated by the feeling of having become like Indians on an American reserve: John Paul II. It seems to me that in almost all these cases the personality becomes simplified, joins up with a type, is summed up in a major feature.

The physiognomy of witnesses one has truly known is very different. Doubtless one prunes the features that one would prefer to ignore or even forget, but what makes its mark is a rounded personality, complex and yet integrated. Here, at the very moment of making this analysis, I feel certain uncertainties that I would like to express without separating them. To begin with, heroism is very attractive; so is generosity which has integrity, whether charitable or ascetic; militancy which absorbs the whole being. However, it is possible that this high tension also contains enough turbulence to deceive those who really approach it and do not have an excessive need simply to keep up appearances. Even if less is promised by a more subdued quality which is also more assured of a welcome, of compassion, of intimate joy, does it not make its mark in the long run? The flame is certainly indispensable – but nothing must be *forced*. Weak points, even lack of balance, may emerge; but they remain localized, without involving, as in the first case, a whole psychology.

In this first dilemma, I have finally come to lean towards one side; in a second my perplexity remains complete. I know that exceptional people – the strong, the rich, the enterprising, the obstinate – are irreplacable; they can exercise more influence than thousands of others put together, and the emanation of witnessing does not escape this law of energy. Even at half-power vigorous or scintillating intelligences and temperaments leave a broad wake behind them. And yet, I am persuaded that in the long term lives, communion, are built up by witnesses whom at first sight one would call 'grey': simple, discreet, ordinary people, laity or the like, known only by those around them (the widow in the temple who strengthens the faith of Jesus!); profound believers, being generous, praying, wounded by the suffering of others, hoping in them, reviving their courage, in spite of their own extreme hesitation to put themselves forward, to express themselves, to profess their faith: blessed, forgiven, at home, luminous, lined up on the threshold of the kingdom and opening wide its gates.

Here are four rather solemn warnings which I do not enjoy writing. First of all, the 'state of perfection' does not exist, the 'religious life' as a specific sign is an illusion and a delusion, and the only 'consecration' to God is that of faith and baptism. However religious we may be, we should expect our witness only to bear fruit to the degree that we are Chrsitians – ourselves, our community – simply, humanly, entirely.

The professional witness is a public and a private menace. Since bearing witness is what holds his life together he *has to* bear witness. And the result is that he lives in the world of the word which does not give way to actions; he knows in advance what everyone must be and therefore cannot hear anyone; he destroys those around him by asking for all to be conformed to their image; he has to pay by proxy the price of his renunciation.

Those who are priests or religious must not imagine that they bear witness in an official capacity: only the weight of their presence counts. Even the worth of what they say is not related to their function but to their person (bishops are different – not because of a sacrament but because of a social power: if they pronounce on a matter of substance, its effect is magnified). Whenever the priest or religious speaks, he must understand that if people will not listen to him in that capacity they would not listen to him in another capacity and he should not be surprised at disappearing into nothingness when he ceases to be what he is. If he loses this little pedestal or launching pad from which he has benefited, will he be in a position to build up new credibility? The amazing thing is that something of the same kind can even be found among non-believers, so marked is the stamp of the clerical model in our culture. Fortunately, once again, the law of witnessing is quite different.

Sometimes there is within us a veiled impulse which leads us to engage in certain forms of abstinence, and then to justify them – but there is also, symmetrically, the demand that others should renounce things, in particular their celibacy. Here again, non-believers are not always spared. Do we have here a need for a fixed social point of reference? Is this a desire for heroism by proxy? Peace at contemplating the end of sexuality? The feeling of possessing something that does not belong to anyone? The maternal role of the celibate priest? Be it what it may, among Christians, as a result of thought-patterns which are developed in religious training, sacrifice has a value in witnessing that is determined by psychological motives. There are so many pitfalls! You may have overcome the emotional, legal or mental prohibitions, but do not underestimate these blockages in others; otherwise you will undermine their faith and come up against all the force of their complexes. Do not overestimate them, either, as you might perhaps have a hidden interest in doing, for that would contribute to the perpetuation of a social lie. There is no easy solution to this dilemma.

Then there are all those who bear witness for others, believers or unbelievers, simply by what they are and possibly by what they say. There are those who are at home in a concern for witnessing and in reflection about it, without believing themselves to be any more convincing as a result. And there are those who are called to pastoral service in the church without being any more or less witnesses than their friends, but helping the witness of others to be born and grow. There are those who feel an imperious vocation to bear witness in season and out of season; but now is no longer the time to cry out at the crossroads; witnessing calls for a gentle hand, a light touch...

Building one another up within the community

There is no prescription for the few basic gospel decisions. Despite the centuries of clericalism, of abbatial paternalism, of masculine tutelage, and so on, the essence of the witnessing relationship in the church remains the mutual help given by one believer to another, in complete equality and reciprocity. It remains in force and, whether one likes it or not, it is the crucial factor, for in this sphere only the reality of beings and their exchanges count. Masks, roles, the trappings of status may impress the simple, but they are not productive, and at heart everyone knows this. To say it again, what we offer is what we are, an exchange in which everyone will discover sooner or later that he has received more than he could give.

One of the forms of this mutual enrichment is listening and giving advice at critical moments or in the daily events of a history of personal faith, which is inalienably the future of a human life with its inner growth to maturity and the external pressures that it withstands. 'Spiritual direction', which is too often the scandalous expression of a will to power and the infantilization of the other, has usurped this brotherly service. But that service is not always simultaneous or bilateral; a certain person, at a certain moment, may help someone else: another day he will find support from a different brother or sister.

I do not rule out the idea of a spiritual paternity, nor the capacity of some people to exercise it for the help of others. But one becomes a spiritual master through a gift and through experience, not by virtue of one's function. We are at the disposal of beginners, so that they can go further. This is only possible with extreme delicacy and must not lead to the abrogation of someone else's responsibility. Even so, one is not a shelter from countless squalls and I would not dare to draw up a list of the best cases among those that I have come across. I myself refuse to play this role, nor do I ask anyone to play it for me.

If we look in almost the opposite direction, it must be said that a certain quality of community life allows each one to receive and to exercise this brotherly help at the right moment, without any inconvenience, either at the heart of general community relationships or on the borders. However, experience always shows that the great crises of existence cannot be negotiated in this way, above all if they involve a change in relationship to the group; in that case one is thrown back on a personal relationship, perhaps external to the community, of the kind I have indicated earlier.

A rather different form of witnessing by word is the noble and no less perilous help that one could call the mercy of truth ('brotherly correction' was drier, in both terminology and content). It is the opposite of welcoming without any preconceived ideas, which is usually the better course, as in the extreme discretion called for in the relationship between Christians and non-believers. But I am sometimes invited by someone to 'tell him the truth', even though this may be hard, and more rarely, I can presume that brotherhood in the faith requires that I should take the initiative. But there are conditions. I must have taken stock to reassure myself as far as possible that this is not a matter of soothing my resentment or even satisfying my conscience. And I must be able to see that such a word has a good chance of being accepted and becoming constructive. Otherwise this magnanimous act turns to the most abject murder: the kind that is committed under the cover of love.

The last form that it seems necessary for me to touch on here is the brotherly service which is performed in religious training, whether catechetical or theological. This is also very different from our relationship with non-Christians to the degree that it involves the transmission of knowledge; but at the same time it becomes the scene of the interplay of forces of power, of social regulation, of clerical ways of thinking or legitimation by a 'tradition'. However, its real effect is in the order of witnessing:

the conviction of faith, the conviction that the instruments of reflection and knowledge which have been handed down have value for Christian life today. The rest is intellectual eroticism, a flight into the past, an illusion of reuniting people, an appetite for power.

In ending this chapter, by force of circumstances, all that is left for me to say is that a great many ways of witnessing rely entirely on words. But so that we do not miss the essential point, it must also be remembered that the mutual support of believers, like their witnessing to non-believers, consists almost entirely in a certain quality of existence. It is that which others discover and which strengthens them; the word arises when it is most natural and most necessary, in order to bring out the theological meaning that we recognize in the life we have sought to live and that we have been allowed to live.

The goal of witnessing

The goal of witnessing is the point reached by the companions of the Samaritan woman when they say that they no longer believe on the basis of what she has said but on the basis of what they themselves have heard. This is an inner conviction, utter autonomy in the faith.

For the witness it is the transition from the bright joy of a beginning to the serene, but controlled, joy of withdrawing in the face of something that has been born and which is growing away.

This victory over self can be renunciation of gratitude, indeed even the acceptance of negation. In any case it will be a somewhat sharp, double lesson: no arrangement about guardianship - whether in connection with a man, a woman, a couple, or growing children – lasts for ever; difference and divergence creep into every feeling of identity.

If there is any room for talking of a failure of witnessing, this must be without judging others, without holding oneself guilty. But when does this actually happen? Is a failure of a religious kind the whole story?

Christian witnessing first of all has a humanizing effect. Young people grow up in a certain way, beings ravaged by life regain hope, and so on. It makes a good deal of sense and has great value as a sign, independently of any religious discovery.

The same thing is true of collective acts and achievements which are inspired by faith and to which faith gives its power of hope: they too count fully, whether one sees them in terms of a history of the rise of humanity or whether one attaches a specific value to them at the point at which they appear, no matter what their future may be.

Every trace of true humanity – or every trace of the gospel, which authenticates it for us -, every spark of goodness or beauty which arises in this world, has an absolute and irrevocable value in its fullness and in its fleeting nature. And is not our hope that God – according to Jesus the God of the living, not the dead - keeps them for ever in his creative memory?

However, the happy ending, the true goal of witnessing, is the dawning of God in a human life.